SECOND

Ultra Violence

**A novel
by
Mark Barry**

Ultra Violence   2nd edition
Published by Green Wizard 2013
© Green Wizard 2013

First published in 2012 by Green Wizard
Green Wizard, Southwell, Nottinghamshire
Greenwizard62@blogspot.com

This book is sold subject to the condition that it shall not by way of trade or otherwise, be lent, resold, hired out, or otherwise circulated without Green Wizard's prior permission and consent in any form of e-transaction, format, binding or cover other than that in which it is published and without a similar condition, including this condition, being imposed on the subsequent purchaser.

Edited by Mary Ann Bernal

Cover design by Dark Dawn Creations

This is a work of fiction. Any resemblance of characters to actual persons, living or dead, is purely coincidental.

ISBN-13:978-1491239483
ISBN-10: 1491239484

Novels by Mark Barry

Carla
Hollywood Shakedown
Kid Atomic
The Illustrated Woman
The Ritual
Ultra Violence
Violent Disorder

Green Wizard Anthology

Reality Bites

Chapter 1

You have never seen this many people, the old city creaking under the strain. Where do they come from? You expect it on a Saturday, but not on a freezing Tuesday in November. You work in Nottingham, and thus, you experience the teeming masses every day, yet the crowded boulevards still have the capacity to surprise you.

You wonder where all the money is coming from. It doesn't make sense. You have heard management is making redundancies in the office - the first time your company has made redundancies for seventeen years. If the rumours are true, then the last thing you would be doing is spending money. Rumours like those ignite squirrel instincts.

The word redundancy tells you to stop spending.

You have read a book about the wisdom of crowds. What you see today is the opposite. Antiwisdom. The city's crowds seem unreasonable, an unthinking host.

Grey sky. An unbroken nebula pregnant with rain. Possibly snow. It feels ready to fall, but the breakthrough moment hasn't arrived and thus, the atmosphere is replete with an almost physical sense of anticipation. There is a sharp wind. It whips around your lips and cheeks, and you are grateful for your overcoat and the thick woollen scarf tucked inside the collars.

You aren't hungry, but you always make sure you take your lunch hour. Plenty of your colleagues work through and let the bosses know it. Mostly the younger ones, brainwashed by American TV. The ones who think they have to work themselves into the ground in order to make a decent life for themselves. The new corporate slaves. The ones who bring an apple for the teacher.

Two young women in Inuit hats and sheepskin boots walk past you. They are both nibbling at jacket potatoes. One of them spills some melted cheese, which creates a suspension bridge between the tray and her top lip. The gooey twine is clearly tricky to shift, and both women chuckle at the hapless attempts at disentanglement.

You hear the trundle of the tram before you see it turn the corner into the Square. You smell fresh hot kebabs from Amigo, nearby. Your mouth waters, but it's much too early for a takeaway.

You walk down Thurland Street, and you see him. Standing outside The Pit and the Pendulum, smoking a fag. You haven't seen him for years.

Beanie. From Notts.

Instinctively, you think that The Pit and the Pendulum, the refurbished Malthouse, an Emo paradise, is an odd place for him to be drinking, but before you know it, the two of you are shaking hands, his grip strong and firm, and his hand dwarfing yours; calloused and engraved from years of brutal labour on the building sites.

Haven't seen you for a long time, youth, he says.

Ages, you say. No matter how old you get, he's still taller than you - and better looking. He smells as if he's been smoking fags. Roll-ups. He's been drinking, and not just the one. It's been a while, you add. Fifteen years?

At least, he says.

That's a long time.

Certainly is, he replies. You stand there briefly awkward as is customary in random reunions like this. Beanie breaks the silence.

What you up to?

I'm on dinner break.

Fancy a swift half? He says. I'll buy.

In here? You look quizzically at him, questioning his pub choice. You never liked the Malthouse in the first place, and you've never been much of a Metalhead.

Two-for-one today, mate, he replies. BOGOF beer, the best type. Good music on the jukebox. None of that X-factor bollocks you hear everywhere else. They played some Zeppelin a bit earlier. Dazed and fucking Confused. Come on, I'll buy.

You shake your head.

Can't drink at dinner, Beanie. Policy.

Bollocks to that. Live a little. He puts his hand on your shoulder firmly. Get you some mints after, he says.

You remember Beanie as one of the best of them, and his appearance inspires a mixture of trust, excitement, and nostalgia. His sheer presence overwhelms and before you know it, you're in the pub, and he's ordering. Two pints of Stella. He's wearing a light blue Arran sweater, fisherman's neck, Levi jeans and a pair of walking boots with striped-red laces. He looks like he should be in the Lake District rather than a city centre boozer, a replica of Satan's Inn.

His hair is longer than you remember it, and it's definitely greyer. His nose has been reddened and pulled apart from drinking too much grog. His cheeks are rough and weather-beaten from a lifetime of outside graft. One of his blue eyes is flecked and yellower than the other. There's a faint smell of last night's party mixed with a decent aftershave. Aramis, you think. A scent you haven't come across since the old days. The aftershave smells to you of nostalgia. He picks up the two pints of beer and gestures toward a staircase. You both descend into a dungeon-style alcove, decorated blood red, as a circle in Hell might look. The alcove is lined with bookshelves full of leather-bound volumes. The shelves surround hardwood tables balanced on sturdy, ornate metal legs. A decent sized fireplace that - sadly for your frozen fingers and toes - isn't lit. If it ever is, with the price of fuel and the price of beer. On the mantelpiece, a gargoyle stares at you. It's a hefty grey slobbering thing with ears the size of a bat, a petrified Imp condemned to guard the Gates for eternity. It watches you into your seat. You suppress a shiver, and you're not sure whether it's due to the cold.

Beanie offers his glass and says cheers. You mirror the gesture.

How are you doing? He asks.

Okay. You?

Not bad. Still going down Notts?

Just home matches and big aways.

City and Sunderland? Fulham? He grins.

Anywhere local. Stags. Spireites.

Do you ever go with the lads? On the coach?

No, you reply, and you feel a bit guilty. Haven't been out with that lot for nigh on fifteen years. You?

Just got back into it. Last two seasons. The Munto thing helped. I'd lost interest in Notts and in any case, I had to work Saturdays. A decent job on the books. Rufty Tufty contracting. Loads of cash - eight hundred, nine hundred quid a week. Couldn't turn that down for football, could I? Paid for most of my house with that, no complaints. Stayed in touch with Haxford and that.

I still see them, you reply, feeling guilty. Just don't do … you know … the same kind of things. Stay out of the road. Park my car. Pay. Sit at the top of the Pavis. Get bored. Leave. Drive home. I took Perry - my lad - down the Lane for years before he lost interest.

Beanie laughs. I remember *you*, you fucker. You were a *proper* nuisance back then.

You experience a delicate sense of embarrassment. That was a long time ago, you reply.

What happened? What made you stop?

I got old. You?

Same. Remember that Forest versus Blades match that was all over the news?

Last match of the season? Ninety-five?

Something like that. The ancient Blades prick that ran on to the pitch to get stuck into A Block.

I remember, you reply. The beer is chilled and refreshing, and although you haven't had more than ten pints in the past year, you find yourself halfway through the pint as if it were iced water on a hot day. That's how it used to be. You used to drink like a fish. Like everyone. It was what you did. For all you know, they still do. Some of them would be in their late forties and fifties.

He was fifty years of age, the knobhead, Beanie continues. Six kids. Ten grandkids. The presiding magistrate couldn't believe what he was hearing in his court. He called him a clown and said he should know better. Then he put him down for six months. I decided there and then that it was time to pack it in. I can't work out which would be worse: Being sent to North Camp, or being shamed in the Evening Post like that.

Has to be the shame. Every time, you reply.

That lot get involved on occasion, Haxford tells me. The latest remaining members of The Should Know Better Club. They were at it at Aldershot last year.

They're about fifty, Beanie. If they're a day.

Proud members of The Should Know Better Club.

You laugh, enjoying the banter.

That's football! A broad church and an addictive one. Another pint? He offers, standing up, glasses in hand.

You are surprised to realise that you want another. The gargoyle looks at you with contempt. You feel a draught coming from one of the bookshelves as if the shelves are hiding a hidden door. A thought comes from nowhere. *The Masque of the Red Death holds sway over all*...then it goes away along with the fleeting wind.

No, not for me, you say. Have to get back to work.

Okay, youth. Still in the same game?

Same company also.

Take my mobile number, he says, pulling out his phone. You exchange numbers. I'm often round town, he continues. Currently exploring the world of unemployment. Changing direction and that. Took a decent redundancy package in a fit of optimism. I'm regretting it.

Tough out there?

You aren't kidding, youth. Haven't had a sniff of a job in months. If you hear of anything, let us know, yeah?

You tell him you will. You both walk up the stairs and shake hands in the doorway.

Whether it's the drink, or the atmosphere, or something else - nostalgia, the modern world - you make a mental note to contact Beanie soon, and go for a beer. You hardly ever go out and seeing him has been a buzz. You feel lightheaded. You stop off at the newsagent two shops down from the Pit and pick up some extra strong mints. You have ten minutes to waste. You walk back slowly to your office.

You sit down at your desk. Remember how it all started.

Best Years of Our Lives

You are thirteen, and it is your turn today.

You don't know why it's your turn today, but you know that it is.

The atmosphere has been building up for weeks.

Those little incidents.

Brief encounters.

Minor skirmishes.

You have never experienced anything like this anticipation before, and you're scared. Your stomach is turning over as if you're staring down the side of a skyscraper. You are tense and dizzy, and you wish you hadn't had seconds at dinner.

Manchester Tart.

Two slices.

You're thirteen, sitting round a school desk, your satchel packed and blazer on.

Five boys are staring at you.

You know it's your turn.

You're paralysed. Panicking. You cannot move. You've never known a feeling like it. Trepidation courses through your veins. Your body is charged, and you want to cry. But you don't. Weeping will only make things worse. You wish it isn't your turn today, but it is. You pray.

That's what they taught you to do at Primary School.

Pray.

When in trouble.

Pray.

God will provide. God will save. They taught you to pray before they taught you to read, those nuns. You really need Him, but as you've long suspected, He isn't there and somehow, even if He *is* out there, you know He isn't going to help.

You're on your own.

You look at the faces of the five boys around your communal table.

You look at the girls sitting round the communal table behind you.

It's planned.

You don't know when they planned it, but they did.

You shut your eyes.

Mrs. Dixon has just given a lesson on punctuation, and you cannot remember anything she has said about full stops, commas, and semicolons because the whole class is staring at you, and they've been staring at you for three quarters of an hour because it is your turn.

Your turn.

Other people have had their turn.

They got to Paul Fisher last week. He still hasn't come back to school.

They got to Clare Finch last month. She had to move classes. Then she had to move schools.

They got to David Gunther two months ago. They say he's gone to a special school. One where they listen to quiet music in class, and there are doctors in white coats, instead of teachers in stinky jackets and polyveldts. It's twenty-seven minutes past three, the old clock above the blackboard tells you. You wonder whether the classes in the surrounding classrooms know it's your turn.

(Please, God.)

They're staring, your classmates.

On Friday nights, as a treat, your mum lets you watch a regular ITV programme called *Appointment with Fear*. Every week, they show an old horror film. *Taste The Blood of Dracula. Frightmare. Dracula, Prince of Darkness. Bride of Frankenstein. Curse of The Mummy's Tomb. The House That Dripped Blood.*

You love horror films. All the old classics.

Plague of the Zombies. The Reptile. Vampire Lovers. Blood Beast Terror. Twins of Evil. Deathline.

You and your mum watch them together, and you drink Horlicks and eat digestive biscuits. Your dad is always in bed asleep, ready for a five o'clock start. He's always working. You've learned that the function of men is to work, and the function of a father is to work harder and to build a home. That's what you've learned.

Scream and Scream Again. Dr Terror's House of Horrors. Asylum. Trilogy of Terror. Dracula Has Risen From The Grave.

You love your mum.

All your friends love your mum because there are no rules in your house. It's open house, and she's a great cook and gives your friends treats and cakes, but the people who come round your house are different friends from another school, closer to where you live. Not the people staring at you now, all from other parts of Nottingham who come in on buses. Bestwood, mostly. Sherwood. Top Valley. You're dad wasn't happy for you to be schooled with all these people, but he couldn't afford to send you anywhere else. Times were hard. He blamed Ted Heath.

Catholics. They're all Catholics from Ireland.

You don't even understand religion, and you don't go to church. You don't believe in God, thinking it's all a bit stupid. Your mum doesn't go, and your dad doesn't go. Your mum is too busy being a mum, and your dad is too busy working. You want to go to a different school, and maybe your classmates detect this. They choose their targets carefully. They choose them for a reason.

Sometimes your mum allows your friends to come to stay and watch *Appointment with Fear*. They don't tell their mums that they're allowed to watch horror films at your house.

Last month, *The Midwich Cuckoos* was on. Sean and Shaun, and Adrian and Barry, and Dominic and Michael, and Francis and James, and Brendan and Peter, and Tom and Fergal are staring at you like the kids in *The Midwich Cuckoos*.

They're sniggering behind their hands. Their blazers on. Regulation white shirts. Oversized, loosely tied, brick-tie knots. Behind you, there is Sheila and Mary, and Annie and Connie, and Margaret and Elizabeth, and Catherine and Jane. Blazers. White blouses. Oversized, loosely tied, brick-tie knots. Lacquered hair and makeup. Giggling behind their satchels.

You are paralysed with fear.

(Please God, make it not my turn. Please save me from this and I'll go to church on Sunday, and forever.)

It's twenty-eight minutes past three and Mrs. Dixon is a stickler for time. She's sitting there putting pens and chalk into her denim bag. You like Mrs. Dixon and you want to tell her what's going to happen, but doing that will only make things worse.

You can only hope that this will be the last time.

You've had warnings.

Francis punched you in the face before PE a week ago and followed it up by stamping on your back. He walked off laughing as if he'd done something to be proud of.

Adrian stabbed you in the hand with a screwdriver.

Keelan approached you in the cloakroom outside the Biology labs while you were finishing off your homework. He gestured to an Adidas bag hanging on a coat hook on the other side of the cloakroom and asked you to come over and look inside. Curious and just a little bit naïve, you got up to see what he wanted you to see. Before you reach the bag, he hits you over the head with a rounder's bat. It is the first time you've been hit on the head like that, and you squeal. You will never forget the sound of the bat rattling on your skull as long as you live, the whiplash cracking, like a snapping plastic ruler. You fall to the floor and bang your forehead on the tiles. It is agony, but it doesn't hurt anywhere near as much as the sound of everyone in the cloakroom laughing at you while you lay on the floor.

Boys and girls. The best years of your life.

That was just the preamble. The beginning.

You are scared this afternoon, and you have never been as scared in your entire life. You want to cry, but you daren't. It will only make things worse.

The bell for home time goes. So does the first ten millilitres of the liquid in your bladder that stains the front of your underpants. You make a run for the door, but Keelan is already by the toilets outside. You don't know how he got there. He punches you and you go down on your knees. He takes advantage of the freedom and space around him to kick you in the face.

They're on you.

Mrs. Dixon can't stop them, how can she, and she walks past into the bright sunlight outside the New Learning Block, into the banks of freshly planted trees and the rolling carpet of the newly turfed school fields.

It is a beautiful sunny, Indian summer day, in nineteen seventy-eight.

You are thirteen.

You are down, your nose hurting from the impact of Keelan's punch. God hasn't helped you. In fact, perhaps to punish you for your lack of faith, He's made your perceptions that much keener. You can see them forming an orderly queue to stick the boot in. You can hear their laughter and smell their excitement. You notice their shoes. The boys are wearing one of three types of shoes.

Shoe type one: Platform soles popularised by glam bands such as The Bay City Rollers, Slade, and T-Rex.

Shoe type two: Cork-soled brogues with a half-moon front, known as Spoons.

Shoe type three: Ordinary leather-soled brogues, also with rounded fronts. Most people in your class are into Northern Soul, and they say these shoes are mint for sliding across polished floors. The relentless impact of the shoes in your face and along your body is wedging you underneath the cloakroom benches, keeping you tight in the confined space. It is making it difficult for you to breathe and impossible to move. You can't even protect your face.

The girls in your class are wearing just the one type of shoe. **Girl Shoe type one**: Leather-stitched moccasins with plastic corn-coloured soles. Mocs, they call them. You notice the sole of one as it crashes down onto your face and you cannot believe that you're being stamped on by a girl.

You realise that all of the girls in your class are kicking you.

They hate you. Boys and girls.

In the first thirty seconds of the attack, you are kicked thirty times and then you lose count.

There is a break from the kicking. Adrian kneels down, picks his spot and punches you. His punch connects with your left eye socket and shuts your eyelid. You have never experienced a jab of pain like it, and it soon turns into a thudding in your forehead.

You can see his face, and it is etched with something.

Hatred. That's what hurts most.

You wonder when Adrian started to hate you. You went to St Francis of Assisi school with him. A nice school with nice teachers. You loved Primary school. Your mum knows his mum. You thought he was a friend. You used to play marbles with him on the playing field running parallel to the classrooms. You used to swap Green Lantern comics.

You competed with him in spelling tests.

I got nine.
I got ten.
I got seven today.
I got eight.
I win!

You don't understand why he's hitting you like this as if he wants to kill you.

As each separate class emerges from the classrooms in the Learning Block, a coagulated, blazered mass of third-year schoolchildren, some break away from the flow to join in the ritual putting in of the boot.

Most of the people hitting you are Forest fans riding high on the back of their European Cup successes. One, who leans on your nose with his knee, has hit you several times before for being a Notts fan. You are outnumbered in the school by ten-to-one, at least. You wonder whether this has anything to do with the beating, or whether it's just religion, or something else you don't understand.

Then you start to black out.

As you're being kicked, the blood pouring from your nose, the pain dulling by the second as you start to lose consciousness, your bladder gone, trails of poo releasing itself under the weight of the beating, something weird happens. Something strange.

You don't know why, or how.

Maybe God is helping you after all because you can feel your fear dissipate.

Before long, you are no longer afraid. The worst they can do is beat you.

You aren't going to die.

You are going to hurt for a month.

Your education is ruined.

You will never have confidence in anything the teachers and nuns at school tell you about life ever again.

You are going to hate all the teachers who failed to protect you.

You are going to hate all the mad, frustrated, ultra-violent people who are beating you without pity, with the intention of inflicting as much pain as possible.

You know that you are going to hate the people in your class forever, *but you aren't going to die.*

This is over.

Your turn is over.

The beating is so bad you know it can never be repeated. They've gone well over the top, the naughty Catholic boys and girls of Corpus Christi school. They've gone laughably over the top, the worst session of Feel The Pain imaginable.

Ho hum.

A teacher emerges from inside the Learning Block to see what the fuss is about. In your confusion, you can't quite place the concerned voice shouting and though his voice is distant, as if you are hearing it through a glass bottle, you see the consequence of his appearance. You know that everyone is running for it, squeezing through the door three at a time, escaping into the sun, leaving you wedged and bleeding under the cloakroom bench.

Two of your classmates, Andy and John, the only two people in your class not to hit you, help the teacher, Mr. Davies, to prise you out, pick you up, and take you into the boy's toilets to clean up. The toilets stink of cigarettes, you notice. All the toilets at Corpus Christi stink of cigarettes and the bowls are never clean.

They cannot understand why you are not crying. You're in agony. Three of your teeth are loose. Your glasses - crappy National Health horse chestnut tortoise shells with springs on the arms - are wrecked, both lenses cracked and the frames twisted, but you don't mind that - you spend most of your school life without glasses, you often break them yourself. Your nose is broken. You can feel it shift and loosen when you touch it. Your ears hurt. Blood drips from the canal of the right ear and you fear they've done some permanent damage. Both eyes are black, and you're lucky not to have broken a socket. Your school shirt is covered in blood. In the mirror, the blood on your shirt looks curiously like the face of Jesus. You lift up your ripped shirt and blazer. Your entire body is covered in yellow bruises inflicted upon you by Spoons, brogues, Northern Soul moccasins, and Glam Platforms. Your legs are stiff, and you can hardly stand. There's a recession on, and your dad is not going to be pleased about having to buy a new blazer, but you're no longer afraid, and although you're in some considerable pain and you find it difficult to move your face, you start to laugh.

That night at home, after the school nurse tells you that you'll be okay, miraculously, you spend the evening taking phone calls from your assailants. Your phone has a lock on the dial to prevent you from calling anyone. At twenty pence a minute, the phone is for emergencies only, dad says. Your mum has the key, but you never ask her to remove the little cylindrical lock nestled on the number seven. You know times are hard, and you're a good lad. You don't burden them.
Please don't snitch, the disembodied voices say.
We're sorry. It all got out of hand. Please don't tell.
We're sorry.
Please don't tell.
It got out of hand.
Adrian calls you, and while you cannot see his face, you know he is scared about what he's done.
His voice is trembling. Please don't tell on me, he says.
None of the girls who kicked you calls. Not even Helen O'Reilly, who stamped on your face. She didn't call even though her brother, Nicholas, has your phone number.
She bent her knee and put her heart and soul into the stamp. You will never forget her blank and merciless face. You learned something about girls you didn't know that afternoon.
I won't tell, Adrian, you hear yourself utter.
I won't tell, Ben, you hear yourself say.
I won't snitch, Kevin, you hear yourself confirm.
There is a concert violinist in your class. There is someone with ambitions to be a doctor. Adrian wants to work in the City of London. You could do some serious damage to their career aspirations. How are they going to

get a job? All three of the people with skills and ambitions laid the boot in.

A doctor? None of it made any sense to you, but, on the other hand, it made perfect sense.

All of them laid the boot in, but you won't tell on them. Your mum is crying and wants to go up to the school and get the teachers - even the police - involved, but you won't let her. You won't tell on them. You have nothing but contempt, and each phone call hardens the contempt further. You hate them, and that hate burns deep into your soul.

Your dad takes you out into the garden when he gets home from work. He proceeds to give you the most important piece of advice you have had up until that point and afterwards, you know that the advice he has given you will last you for the rest of your life.

Son, if you can't beat them, join them, he says.

You can see in his face that he's tired after another twelve-hour shift at the brewery. He works six days a week, sometimes seven. The only time you see him for more than an hour is either at the match on Saturday afternoon, when Notts are at home, or on Sunday afternoon, asleep in his vest, snoring on the sofa, with Star Soccer on the telly, and four cans of Double Diamond on the occasional table next to him, the smell of Sunday lunch in the ether. They never show Notts on Star Soccer, he's fond of saying. They *definitely* never show Notts on Match of the Day.

You love your dad. He would never lie to you. *If you can't beat them, son. Join them.* You are surprised at this advice, but still, you sense a door opening to a different world.

Thanks, dad.

You're welcome, son.

Chapter 2

The next day, you arrive back from lunch, take off your suit jacket, and place it on the back of your chair.

The company intranet homepage greets you and asks for your username and password. Your username is Oakes, after a skilled Notts playmaker, one of the few bright spots in a horror decade where the Magpies almost went out of business.

A white vellum envelope addressed to you rests on your keyboard. Four co-workers work in the same office, but they're all out at lunch. Only the sound of cars travelling down Broad Street disturbs the silence.

You open the envelope. Remove the letter.

You read the letter.

Then you read it one more time.

The letter is from Margot Pearce, the manager your company has imported from Shrewsbury to replace Dave, your boss of twenty years.

You put down the letter.

You have an appointment in Mansfield at three, and you turn off your PC. You leave a note on Rupert's desk telling him you won't be back. You live in Mapperley, and it is pointless coming back into the centre of town after an hour meeting in Mansfield. You put on your suit jacket and pick up your raincoat. You walk down three flights of stairs to the car park. Jane Pickles passes you and says hello, but you ignore her.

You don't mean to. Ordinarily, you're polite and friendly, and she's a top woman, one of the good ones. A short time later, you pull yourself together on the way up through Sherwood, and you realise what you've done.

The meeting goes poorly.

You consider yourself lucky to retain important business. You breathe a sigh of relief to have survived.

You arrive home at six because the heavy Nottingham traffic is even worse than usual. You park your car in the garage and enter the house. Shout hello to Rita, your wife. She's on the phone to someone and doesn't respond. You shout upstairs to your son, Perry. You know he's in because you can see his hoodie and book bag hanging on the staircase. His trainers with the big luminous pink laces lie askew on the carpet.

You share cooking duties with Rita. Tonight, it's her turn, but there is no smell of cooking food. The kitchen is identical to the one you left behind this morning. Cereal bowls half full. Toast crusts scattered on plates. Half-empty cups of tea. A free newspaper turned to an article about a new species of dinosaur discovered in Chinese mountains.

The radio is on - commercial radio, unlistenable - and you turn the channel over to Radio Nottingham. You switch on the half-empty kettle, sit down, and listen to the news. Youth unemployment reaches a million. The Euro is on the brink of collapse. Dissidents demonstrate in Syria, Egypt, and the Yemen and in each, the State cracks down, leaving protesters dead on sandy squares. There is drought in Asia. Commentators blame ongoing clear-cut deforestation. Cue fierce Indonesian counter claims of propaganda.

Impressario Simon Cowell sacks the X Factor favourite for various abuses of his contract, all of which involve women and drugs. In local news, magistrates send the nephew of Evening Post bogeyman, Colin Gunn, to prison. City Council leaders complain about the protest camp in the Square and want talks. The presenter starts talking about Forest. You stand up, turn off the radio knowing that afterwards, there will be ten seconds on events at Meadow Lane.

Ten seconds tops.

Rita is still on the phone by the sound of it. There is no sign of Perry.

You make yourself a cup of tea and read the letter. You can't quite believe what you read earlier. You were distracted and offhanded in your meeting in Mansfield, and it's a good job you know Daniel and Jane well. Some of the mistakes you made were an embarrassment. Newer partners would have reached for the phone and called competitors.

You know Margot doesn't like you and the letter proves it.

She's new school, thirty-five, a graduate in Business Studies, one of the new breed of Apprentice-inspired female managers with a degree, a well cut suit, expensive shoes and a point to prove. Head Office transferred her to your branch to oversee a management transition. She likes Nottingham that much she decided to make the city her permanent base. In the recruitment round, you are the only qualified person who didn't put in a management application and because of this (the word is), she thinks that you are unambitious, lack commitment and are set in your ways.

"Coasting and loafing." Rupert told you she said that.

Coasting and loafing.

That's what you've been doing for the past year, according to Margot. No room for coasters and loafers in a branch run by Margot Pearce, according to Rupert.

In fact, you don't want to be a manager. Too much paperwork, too much responsibility and backstabbing night and day by the suits higher up than you. Management is a poisoned chalice. You're happy in your work, and as far as you're concerned, you're good at it.

Initial introductions with Margot were not good. She was cold as ice, no hint of a smile on her thin, perfectly worked out and meticulously made-up face.

These things happen. You didn't hit it off. Something non-verbal. Maybe you remind her of someone.

She laughs and jokes with Rupert, John, and Sheila.

It's just you. You have never been paranoid.

It's just you.

You're the longest serving employee, you're the oldest, and you're very well paid. That might have something to do with it.

You lean back and take stock.

The letter says that you are to attend a disciplinary hearing. Next week. A customer has complained about something you did. The letter doesn't lay out precisely the nature of the charge. It could be Gross Misconduct. That's instant dismissal. Margot is chairing the panel. You are permitted a witness, someone from Human Resources, or a friend. The words burn like acid in your soul. You scratch your temple and stare in disbelief. You can't even begin to think where the alleged misdemeanour occurred and what it might be. A moment of panic descends. Your heart races. The full extent of the situation hits like a hammer on the head of a nail

Losing your job is a possibility. Losing your job is something you don't want to happen.

You are well into your forties. Going grey at the temples.

You have an Achilles Heel: A debilitating stomach illness that recurs roughly every two months leading to unavoidable sick leave. Two years ago, you spent more time in hospital than you did at work. Dave, your old boss, tolerated that because he was loyal as a bloodhound. You needed him to be, and you returned the favour whenever you could. You worked well with Dave and you miss him. You have a set of skills specific to the company you work for. There are competitors who could use those skills, but you know that they aren't recruiting. Widespread unemployment and large numbers of slavering graduates straining at the leash mean that professional recruitment rounds are keenly contested. It isn't going to be easy to find another job if Margot gives you the bullet.

Your job is worth thirty-three thousand pounds per year without bonus. Add another four for that. Plus car allowance and five weeks holiday.

It's a good job. You know everyone. You're part of a family, one of the lads, part of the furniture. You're loyal and intelligent. You're generally popular, and you enjoy what you do.

Now, some career-obsessed know-nothing in patent high-heel shoes is about to take it away from you. You feel a flash of anger and bitterness, and you could quite happily drive to work tomorrow and have it out with her.

Get it all out in the open.

A frank exchange of views.

Rita comes into the kitchen and without saying hello, picks up her coat from the back of the chair.

I have to go out, she says.

But it's your turn to cook, you reply.

Sorry. Emergency. Sis is having a crisis.

Sis is always having a crisis.

Family. Have to be there.

Family? What am I!?

She looks at you in an undecipherable way, halfway between indifferent and vacant. Almost imperceptibly, she shakes her head, and she's walking away from you.

I'll see you in a couple of hours. Chippy's down the road, she says to you on the way out.

Rita, you shout, but she's already out the door.

You could have done with talking to her. You're full of angst that feels like fire in your stomach. Head spinning. Margot is stitching you up, and you're scared. There's no beer in the fridge. You climb the stairs to see if Perry wants anything to eat. You knock on his door. There's no answer. You open it. Perry is on his X-Box 360 playing a war game. He has his headphones on, and he's laughing and joking, talking to other players from around the world. He doesn't see you. You tap on his shoulder, and he flinches, spins round.

What?

I'm going to the Chippy. Do you want anything?

No.

Are you sure? You can have anything you want.

Don't want anything. Shut the door on your way out, he replies, turning back to the screen.

Perry is fourteen, and at one time, he was the best friend you had. Now he can scarcely bring himself to look at you. You embarrass him, and at times, you even think he hates you. Sullen, bad-mannered, violent-tempered and dismissive are accurate descriptions of his current personality. It seems to you that one day Perry went to school, an episode of *Invasion of the Bodysnatchers* occurred, and an evil alien hosted by Perry's body returned in his place. He plays computer games and listens to hard-core rap music all night. He won't come to Notts because they're "crap" and all his friends follow Forest, or teams that exist only on television like Man United or Chelsea. The pair of you used to go to Meadow Lane all the time. Notts embarrass him now.

You thank your lucky stars that he doesn't follow Forest.

That would be the end. Whatever indoctrination had passed from father to son was still working. You couldn't face Perry following Forest. Not for a second.

You couldn't imagine following anyone else.

Notts are in the blood.

You sit down on your armchair, and you remember the moment it all changed for you.

Blue Orc

You are fourteen. Notts, the team you support now and forever, are playing Cardiff City at Meadow Lane. The dilapidated ground bathes in bright sunshine.

Some of the Notts supporters around you are bare-chested, soaking up the sun.

Everyone is in good spirits. It is the last match of the season, and a good crowd is in. The football season is ending. A three month break. Your dad says this is a ritual, the last match. He had been offered overtime at the brewery today, but he says he doesn't like to miss the last match. He turned it down.

He tells this same tale every season.

A ritual.

Whenever your dad isn't working, he takes you down to Meadow Lane. The two of you stand on the roadside on the concrete stepping near the half-way line. Your dad drinking tea, in his suede jacket and blue jeans, his thick Jason King moustache and long hair. You've got your light blue Adidas tee-shirt on, with the three dark blue stripes, and you're wearing the woolly black and white scarf your Aunty Theresa knitted for you around your neck. She even knitted **Magpies,** in white, on one of the black stripes near the bottom, just above the tassels.

You come from a long line of Notts County supporters, and you're proud to continue the tradition. You hate school and cannot wait for it to end. Going to see Notts is the most exciting part of the week. You look forward to the next match from the moment the final whistle draws the curtain on the most recent game.

You, as your dad says, are football mad. You collect all the cards and stickers in an album. Each year, you create your own football league ladder from the kit SHOOT provides. You go to bed thinking about football and you wake up thinking about football.

Today, there are ten thousand people in the old ground and the atmosphere is particularly raucous. Everyone is clapping and singing, particularly the band of Magpies underneath the wooden shed on the Roadside.

They're making a rare old noise, chanting a variety of songs. You join in most of them.

Super Notts!
Super Notts!
C'mon You Pies!
C'mon You Pies!
Oh, Notts County - the only football team to come from Nottingham.

Cardiff City supporters have filled their corner of the Kop. The last match of the season means a good away turnout, considering neither side has anything to play for. Their supporters are singing back, but their songs are less about encouragement and more about insulting the English.

They hate English people. Dad says some of the most vicious supporters in the country follow Cardiff City, and he wished they were fenced in, but they are not. Many grounds around the country had decided to put up fencing, to keep the fans from invading the pitch and worse, fighting with each other, but Meadow Lane had held back.

Money, your dad says. Notts can't afford it.

He tells you that since Stoke City destroyed the Main Stand in the last match of last season, the Board had discussed fencing, but had decided that it was too expensive and that stand repairs were the priority. You remember watching Stoke supporters rampage that day. Ten thousand celebrating promotion. They smashed the steps of the Kop into rubble and threw the debris at players and the home fans. They climbed the lighting pylons. They ripped out the benches in the Main Stand. Some even attacked Notts *players* on the pitch, five minutes before the end. And Stoke was winning. They rampaged throughout the stadium. They tried to get into the Notts changing room. Jimmy Sirrel, Notts County's legendary manager, came at them with a knife and a broken beer bottle.

Animals, he called them. *Animals.*

They wrecked the Boardroom, robbed the drinks cabinet, ate the Director's buffet, pee'd on the boardroom flowers, tore famous old photographs and memorabilia from the walls, wrecked the furniture, intimidated and attacked every member of Meadow Lane staff they encountered. They hurled the club cat from the top of the building onto the Director's car, (luckily, it survived). They smashed car windows - around the stadium, there wasn't a car with a windscreen left intact. They beat up any Notts fan that got in their way (some seriously, your dad mentioned gravely).

The police seemed powerless to stop them. Any policeman who tried to intervene was battered. You didn't see any of this because with ten minutes to go, your dad got you out of the situation as fast as he could.

Dad mentioned that up until that day, Notts had largely missed the hooligan cult sweeping football and had become complacent. Stoke supporters caused thousands of pounds worth of damage. The Board was distraught with the close season coming up and zero revenue coming into the club during the cricket season.

You decided at that moment that you didn't like Stoke City.

The consensus on the terraces was that it had not been a bad season at Meadow Lane. While Forest carry all before them over the Trent, you and ten thousand others ignored them and focused on the object of your love. The referee blows for the final whistle. The players shake hands and all the kids invade the pitch the second the whistle is blown. You are among them. You arrange to meet your dad at the corner of the Meadow Lane stand. You join the rush and all the kids run energetically toward the centre circle. You try to pat as many players on the back as you can. Don Masson is your favourite. Ian Scanlon. Steve Carter. Brian Stubbs. Les Bradd - the finest centre forward since Tommy Lawton, but in the end, there are too many people and you don't reach anyone.

You don't expect to see what you see, but you see it, nonetheless.

Coming toward you is a giant troll.

A troll.

You've been reading *Lord of the Rings* after school and the thing coming toward you is how you imagine an Orc to look, but you know that an Orc is just a troll by another name. A troll.

He is as old as your dad is. A skinhead.

His face painted blue. He's wearing dungarees with turn-ups nearly up to the knees and a pair of Doc Marten boots. Eighteen holes, burgundy. He has no top on underneath the apron of his dungarees, and he has two blue and white scarves around each wrist. His troll arms are covered in tattoos. Spider's webs. Birds. Words difficult to decipher. The Welsh national flag. The initials CCFC. His head seems inflated and much too big for his body. His eyes stick out on stalks, and his neck is almost purple, scabbed and cabled, like a burn victim. He has five gold studs on the lobe of his left ear. One of the studs, bigger than the rest, is a grinning skull.

The troll is coming toward you. All the kids around you stop chasing players and scatter because there are more of them, ten trolls, twenty trolls, thirty trolls and they're racing across the pitch toward the Notts supporters. The troll with the scarves around his wrist is seemingly coming toward you, especially you, and your blood turns to water.

You don't run.
You use your head.
He's a man. Not a boy.

He isn't going to hit you.

The troll comes up to you and goes "Boo" in your face. He stinks of beer, cigarettes, and meat pie. His face is pale as if he's about to be sick.

On each of the fingers of his right hand, there is a letter. B L U E tattooed with a hot biro and printer's ink.

On each of the fingers of his left hand, there is a letter. B I R D.

He runs past you.

You stay stock-still.

You turn around, the crowd swaying one way, then another. You look over to where you are going to meet your dad. In the corner of the Roadside stand, there is fighting between the men of Notts County and the Cardiff trolls. It's straight out of Middle Earth.

You can tell them apart.

Notts much less decorated and painted, mostly wearing NCB issue donkey jackets, or green jackets with orange lining, or all denim outfits. Most of them are skinheads – however, there are a few Notts who look like Noddy Holder and Marc Bolan.

The fighting is vicious with neither side taking control. Instead of running away like a sensible lad, you run toward it, to get as close as you can and watch. The police are struggling to preserve order. You watch excitedly. The punches go in thick and fast. There are shouts and curses, people gathering round, some joining in, opening a second front that the Cardiff fans are happy to confront. They whirl their arms, shouting and exhorting. The trolls are an organic helicopter of whirring boots and crashing punches. If someone went down, he was kicked, like you were at school that time, the men putting the boot in, a feeding frenzy. If he stood up, he was punched or butted. This wasn't play fighting, and if you were in the middle of it, you got some. There was no escape in the melee.

You watch the brawl open-mouthed.

You feel the tension around you, hundreds of people excited. You hear the war cries, the squeals of pain, and the entreaties. You watch them go back, and the next minute go forward, a constantly shifting mass, like wheat in a field buffeted by a confused wind.

You feel something happen to your body, something unusual. You look down and something strange has happened between your legs. You don't understand it. You are embarrassed, and you cross them, put your hands down to cover up. You look round and hope your dad hasn't seen you. You don't want your dad to know. That would be embarrassing. Your head is hot and ready to burst and for you, the fight could go on forever. You only wish you were older and could join in the fighting.

More police come over, and the fight breaks up, fans everywhere. A Cardiff troll is dragged away in front of the goal posts, a policeman holding each arm. Instead of being horrified, as you would be, the troll is laughing.

Why would you laugh at going to prison?

Your dad appears at your side.

C'mon, son, let's go. I'll get us some fish and chips back in Arnold. Let's leave these beasts to it.

Yes, dad. You say it with disappointment. You love fish and chips, and you love your dad, but you want to stay and watch the aftermath.

Your dad is strong, and he's guiding you away.

You look at his face, and you wonder whether he has seen the glint in your eye.

In Arnold, he has said to you regularly, there are just the five career options.

Factory.

Pit.

Army.

Sixth form, or college.

If you're really thick, catering college.

He tells you that you're going to make the best of yourself. O' levels. A' levels. Get out of this place and see the world. University.

Yet after seeing what you'd just seen, after experiencing what you'd just experienced, you knew without any doubt that what *you* wanted to be, not what your dad wanted you to be, was a football hooligan.

University was the furthest thing from your mind.

You couldn't wait to come down to the match on your own.

You hope your dad didn't see those thoughts in your eyes, but you suspect he did.

Chapter 3

Hurt - you can't help but feel like that - you pick up your raincoat and take a slow walk in the freezing cold up to Mapperley Top to get chips. You're starving and miserable. You feel empty. You walk up several streets in winter weather. Night, a hint of snow in the air and a bitter wind from the East beginning to whip up. You decide to take a shortcut through the car park behind the supermarket.

There are no cars in the car park. Some of the lights are out of action, and the open space of the car park is forbidding. The area is surrounded on all sides by razor-wire-topped walls and the backs of shops. Two young men sit on the wall lining the jitty leading to the chip shop. Deep as you are in your own thoughts, you barely notice them. You barely notice them even when they're in front of you, one of them pointing a knife, a silver blade that flashes in the tepid glow of the amber streetlights.

Shadowy figures, more ghost than human. Obscured faces because their hoods are up - hoods as deep as monastic cowls, dark scarves over their mouths. Their nervousness transfers and mutates around the three of you standing there in the darkness.

They're shaky, unsure of themselves - this action may even be spontaneous - and their shakiness makes you stand absolutely still. You make no movement. Your blood turns to iced water. You don't even blink.

Predators and prey.

You realise that you're in danger.

Gissit, one of them says.

What?

Gissit! He gestures with his knife.

What?

Don't fuck about. Gisyerwallet, yeh.

You're wasting your time. I have about a tenner on me. That's for my dinner.

One of them punches you.

You've had worse punches in the old days, but that was another time, another era. You're fat and unprepared. These young men can't be more than eighteen. They're lean and fit, and you don't have a chance. If you run, they'll catch you and open you up like a tin of beans. If you resist, they'll open you up like a tin of beans.

Okay, okay! You open your raincoat and hold up your hands. Here's the wallet. That's all there is.

You reach into your inside pocket and hand over your wallet. A flash memory of a film called *Death Wish* - where the protagonist, Charles Bronson, finding himself in the same situation, pulls out a gun - comes to you. You wish you had a gun because you would definitely use it. There's about forty quid in the wallet plus cards, which you're going to have to cancel. Bastard!

Where's your pad, businessman?

What? You're struggling to understand their dense Jamaican/Nottingham hybrid patois.

Your pad, Babylon Boy, your pad. You white men in suits always got a pad for business. Keep your business tings in order, innit.

I've left everything at home...

Another punch from the same boy lands on your nose and knocks you over, a good one this time. He's not wearing gloves. He bends over you and presses the flat edge of the blade into your cheek. He's breathing heavily, almost hyperventilating. You can see his eyes. He's up close and scared shitless. No idea what he's doing. This makes you feel strangely calm. You remember.

(We all have to die sometime...)
(It's your turn.)

You're being beaten and mugged, and you've had worse.

(He's a shitter. He's shitting it, look.)

You're bleeding onto your shirt, the sparse illumination and the rainfall splashing on the car park giving the landscape an almost peaceful ambience.
(I'm going to die, and I'm not scared. I'm not afraid...)

You hear a voice.
Oi! Oi!
The muggers turn round to look.
Someone sprints up the jitty, a rare public-spirited citizen with bottle. The two boys make a run for it down into Carlton. They are fast and it's pointless thinking about chasing them. They will have faded into the ether in seconds. They weren't stupid - they had the presence of mind to keep the wallet.

The man is vaguely familiar.
He's your age. In a black Adidas tracksuit and New Balance running shoes.
He offers you a hand, and you take it, pick yourself up.
Alright, mate? He asks.
Thanks to you, I am.
You recognise the voice. A strong Nottingham accent.
Glad to help.
I'm glad you did.
You're the third this month. This place is lethal.
I won't be coming back through here.
Maybe it's even the same lads.
They didn't look like pros to me. They looked scared.
Did they get anything? He asks.
Wallet. Forty quid, you reply.
I'd give the info to the cops.
Listen, do I know you from somewhere?
I have the same feeling about you, mate, he replies, laughing. You Forest or Notts?
Notts.

So am I! Maybe that's it. Not been down for a while - they're fucking shit this year! - but I reckon I've seen you about.

I'll bet that's it.

Hah! I'll bet it is.

The pair of you stand there chatting for a few minutes, but in that time, neither of you can place the other.

Eventually, your saviour tells you he has to dash. You shake hands before he runs off into the night.

Weirdly, neither of you thought introductions were necessary. No-one bothers with names nowadays.

The last thing you feel like doing is eating, and you know that in ten minutes, you're going to go into delayed shock. Even though you have a fiver in your raincoat, enough for a bite to eat, you turn back and walk home. You do not intend to call the law - what can they do? - but you'll be spending the next hour on the phone to various call centres.

You realise that you've had better days.

That night, as Rita snores lightly next to you, you dream and dream vividly. In the morning, you remember your dream. You sit up on the pillow, and you remember. You don't know why you dreamt of what you dreamt of, but you did.

Chelsea 1981

Chelsea away. Nineteen eighty-one.

You are fifteen-years-old and in the final year of school. If Notts win this game in West London, they will be promoted to Division One. That would be the most amazing thing ever. A chance to play the big outfits every week. Liverpool. Man United. Everton. All the teams they show on Match of the Day. Notts would be in Shoot and Match Weekly. The players would be famous.

Better, it would be a chance to compete with your rivals, Forest.

It is the most important match in Notts County's recent history, and you decide that you *have* to be there.

This posed a problem. You have no job outside a paper round and no way of getting to Chelsea without your dad paying for a train trip and a match ticket. The idea of Notts being promoted to the elite without you being there is something you cannot bear.

Over Weetabix and beaming smiles, you ask whether he can take you to Chelsea.

He says no.

I'm working, he says.

Please, dad.

No. I'm working. I have to pay for the summer holiday. We're going to Benidorm, and I need to work all the overtime I can get.

But it's Chelsea…Notts…

You'll have many more chances to see Notts promoted.

Can I go on my own? You implore, widening your eyes like a hungry puppy.

No. You're too young.

But I'm fifteen, you say.

Thus, you go to work on your dad.

For two weeks, it goes on like this.

You are relentless.

By the Friday before the match, you have badgered, cajoled, harassed, wound and blackmailed your father to the point of insanity.

You pick your spots.

If he's on the early shift, you get up with him and have breakfast. Like an eager dog wagging his tail, you are there waiting for him behind the front door when he gets home from work. No task is ever denied. You mow the lawns. You help him tidy the garage. You wash the Cortina until it shines like an exploding sun. Accompanying each good deed and kindness, is a reminder about the match in West London.

You give him reasons. You mention a rite of passage.

Like a bar Mitzvah or your Confirmation. You tell him it would be good for your education to see London. You promise to visit the Tower of London and the Houses of Parliament. You promise to pop in to the Imperial War Museum and the Natural History Museum. You say to him that you will bring back guidebooks.

You are The Executioner.

Your mission is paramount, and you never stop until your mission is completed.

You must get to Stamford Bridge. No other outcome is acceptable.

It is Stamford Bridge, or it is death.

Finally, out of sheer exhaustion, your father agrees to let you go.

You hug him, and he looks awkward. You suspect your mum has had something to do with the success of the mission. You wouldn't have had to badger mum. She always lets you do what you want. That's the advantage of being an only child. You see your mum hovering over the cooker, removing hot scones from the oven. She doesn't engage your look, but you know she is smiling inside.

There is a tablet of commandments.

No sneaking in pubs and drinking. No scarves. Chelsea are known to be the second most violent thugs in the country, he tells you. If they know you are a Notts fan, they will give you a kicking.

Leave your scarf at home.

You are to blend in. Speak to no one. Especially anyone from Nottingham. That will just make their hooligans think you are part of a gang.

You will go down on the train.

You will take the tube.

You will come straight back after the game.

He tells you that he will pick you up at the station at nine pm. If you are not there, he says, he will call the police.

Make sure you catch a train between six and seven in the evening. There are plenty of trains travelling north, he tells you.

He says nothing to you about historical monuments, but you decide to go and see some anyway. The idea of London thrills you as much as the match, in many ways. You've only been once before, and you were too young to appreciate it. On the morning of the match, dad wakes you up and gives you your money for the trip. Your mum hugs you, and he drops you off at the 20 bus stop on his way to work. He is unsmiling as he lets you out of the car. You can see the bus coming in the rearview mirror.

Your father puts his hand on your shoulder.

Be careful down there. Remember what I said. Blend in. Don't make yourself conspicuous. Understand, son?

Yes, dad. The bus is coming.

His grip on your shoulder is firm, and he has a look of concern on his face, the like of which you have never seen before.

Promise me. Don't stand out and come straight back.

Yes, dad.

The bus is nearly at the stop. It's a bright morning, and you cannot wait to get going. You're fifteen, and you do not need this display of concern. You can handle yourself. You're an adult.

Promise me. I mean it, he says.

I promise, dad. Now can I get the bus? I'll miss my train.

And whatever you do, if someone asks you the time, just run.

Really, dad?

Definitely, son. Never tell someone the time at a place like Chelsea.

He releases his grip on your shoulder and grins, the moment of angst dissipated as fast as it arrived.

Have a great day, son. And get a programme. I wish I were coming.

You get out of the car and put your hand out to signal the olive green double-decker to stop. You are the only passenger catching the bus and if you hadn't have gotten out of the car when you did, the bus would not have stopped, and you would have had to wait for half an hour for another.

On the concourse outside Fulham Broadway underground station, you have never seen this many people in your life.

Thousands of people. Thousands.

They are all Chelsea.

You walk to the stadium in a snake-like procession. There is a hubbub, a level of chatter existing just below the threshold of perception. Hundreds of cars line the Fulham Road, westbound past the stadium.

You have taken your first train trip to London, and now you are at Stamford Bridge.

You have never been as excited.

The excitement started the minute you caught the Inter-City 125 train to London at Midland Station. It continued when you walked into the centre of London, stopping off for a breakfast at a café full of Greeks. It carried on when you saw the sights you wanted to see. Buckingham Palace. The Houses of Parliament. Nelson's Column. St Paul's Cathedral. It moved up a gear the minute you got off the tube at Fulham Broadway.

Strange smells assail you.

You walk past shops offering Shish Kebabs and Doners and Humus. You have no idea about this food and you are awed. You wish you had unlimited money and a London accent because you'd go and try a Shish. Where you come from, it's all fish and chips. Here, in the metropolis, there are Italian places, Indian places and Chinese places. Newsagents sell the New York Times and Le Monde on racks full of publications. There are pubs everywhere and inside they are jammed, drinkers spilling out onto the road, queues to get in. Both pavements are full, and progress is slow. Smelly burger vans line the road, big brothers to the box-like stalls that block the procession. The burger vendors are doing brisk business and although you are hungry, speaking would reveal your origins, and you've promised to blend in. You are invisible. As yet, no one has noticed you.

The Executioner's stealth mission proceeds successfully.

Your dad doesn't buy burgers or hot dogs from the vans outside Meadow Lane. He says they are filthy, and that attitude has rubbed off on you. He told you a story when you were young, which included black fingernails, tongues, dog hairs and an upside-down egg. You will never forget that story - you were too young for it to wash over you and it imprinted. Instead, you'll wait to get inside the ground and have pie and Bovril.

Most of the young Chelsea fans are wearing Greenjackets and Doc Martens. Skinheads of all sizes. Fat skins. Lean skins. Squat skins. Occasionally, a chant will start up from somewhere up ahead.

Chelsea! Chelsea!
Chelsea! *Chelsea!*

Outside a pub called the Kings Head, you see ten or eleven blokes raise their pint glasses and start to sing a song you've never heard before at the Lane.
I go out.
I drink ten pints.
I get really plastered.
I go out and beat the wife.
Coz I'm a Northern bastard.
Some sing this with a grin on their face. Some don't. They repeat the verse and start to do the Moonstomp. They sing another song, but you can't hear the words because the pressure on the pavement pushes you along toward the ground, which you can see up ahead.
Stamford Bridge.
Your dad has taken you away before. Forest, of course. The Baseball Ground. Filbert Street. Field Mill. Sincil Bank. You've been to Loftus Road to see Notts lose 5-1 versus QPR, a side featuring your hero, Don Masson, the brilliant Stan Bowles, Gerry Francis, Dave Clement, the majestic Rodney Marsh. They tore Notts to pieces with football you had never seen before, football imported from another planet. You've been to Old Trafford and been pelted with coins as you waited for the football special to return to Nottingham. You've stood on a banked terrace at Molyneux so vast, you could not see its beginning or its end.

Stamford Bridge is different.

This is your first away match alone, and this is the biggest match.

There's something at stake - a place in Division One.

It's something special. You take a deep breath.
Stamford Bridge.
It fills your eye, and you pull away from the crowd and stand just off the kerb to take it all in. You are filled with a sense of amazement. You see the giant pylons.

The West Stand, which almost reaches the sky. Behind that you know, is the Shed.

The famous Shed.

What could be better than this?

Notts at Stamford Bridge.

You decide to watch the match from the terraces next to the Shed. Shrewdly, you have worked out that joining the Notts fans would just mark you out as a target. You're not much of a cheerer and shouter; you'll blend in anywhere. All you need to do is keep your mouth shut. There is a queue for the turnstiles. You detect a faint hint of piss in the air mixed with the smell of frying onions. All the men around smell of beer and cigarettes. Those just in front of you are drunk, and they sway as they talk. They are your dad's age, have long hair, and look like characters from The Sweeney, one of your favourite programmes. One wears a purple car coat, trousers and loafers. He sways as he speaks.

Haven't seen many Northern cants.

They've faccing bottled it, Norris. They won't come dahn ere. Not to Chelsea.

They only need a point. I faccin wouldn't miss that.

Northern cants. Shitters. They're different, you know that. Faccing warped. Shagging their sisters. Who the facc are Notts County...

They continue in this vein as the slow queue snakes to the turnstile. They are laughing, and you realise that they are trying to outdo each other, see who can come up with the most offensive description of Northerners. You feel angry inside, but you are surrounded by Chelsea fans. What can you do to defend your honour? You realise that you have not seen a Notts fan since the train down. They are doing the same kind of blending that you are.

The ground is rammed and you find a spot out of the way up near the top of the terrace. A birds-eye view. The emerald-green pitch etched with chalk lines, like neat crop circles. The ground is incomplete, and there are gaps. It looks better from the outside, and you are surprised.

You see the Shed to your right. It is an impressive sight. Soon, thousands and thousands of men in green jackets are doing the Moonstomp as the teams come out on to the pitch. The terrace you are standing on is not overly full and luckily, it is full of middle-aged men and their children, like you and your dad. It seems all the skinheads are in the Shed, and the West Stand, and in the stand opposite you, where the little knot of Notts fans are, surrounded by rubble, empty space, policeman and the animosity of the locals.

You clap non-specifically at anything, paranoid. You look at your programme, and you keep your head down. You don't know how or why, but you detect a change in the atmosphere as if your presence is somehow wrong, as if you shouldn't be there. You are nervous, and all of a sudden, you wish your dad was there. You think of the other Notts fans in the ground. You wonder if they feel like you. Having to hide their loyalties and their accents. Not being able to cheer. Knowing that one false word out of place could mean a serious beating.

The minute the match kicks off, the atmosphere turns from anticipation, to hate, viciousness and bile, and you have never experienced anything like it. The hatred is tangible. The Shed goes to work. Nazi salutes whenever Harkouk and Pedro get the ball. Monkey chants. The Northern bastard song. The Moonstomp. The noise is deafening. Chelsea nearly score and everyone around you starts to sing.

Chelsea! Chelsea!
Chelsea! Chelsea!

Someone - your age - turns round and stares. He is wearing a purple jumper, jeans and white tennis shoes. You've never seen anyone dressed like him at a match before. His hair is parted to one side, like an old-fashioned Dandy, like a picture of Oscar Wilde. He turns away.

He is joined by two or three other boys your age, all dressed identically.

Bright colours. Jeans. White trainers.

Purple Sweater says something to his friends and they all look round at you.

You start to panic inside.

They are going to ask you the time.

They know.

They know.

You look at your programme. They don't look like hooligans.

Not like Cardiff.

They look more like *posh* kids.

They start to walk up the terrace toward you.

You remember.

(It's my turn.)

Just at that moment, Trevor Christie scores.

You suppress the urge to cheer. Only the small knot of Notts fans over in the other stand congratulate the scorer, and you can't hear them. The Chelsea fans go wild, those in the Shed attempting to storm the pitch. The boys in front of you turn, and along with everyone else, run down to the front of the terrace and attempt their own mini-pitch invasion.

You seize the moment, walk round the top of the terrace, pushing past gesticulating and shouting people. They don't notice you - too busy swearing at the referee. You have only one choice because those boys know that you are a Northern bastard, and they are going to ask you the time, and then they are going to kick the shit out of you. They will do this even though they look posh, and you walk down briskly to the concourse where the turnstiles are.

You don't know how they spot you, but they do. They come walking along the fence at the front, in their bright jumpers, and you ask a man in a donkey jacket standing next to a turnstile whether he can let you out because you are not feeling well, and he gives you a knowing grin and you look behind you, and the four boys are running and shouting something, and the man in the donkey jacket takes his time about opening the gate, and the boys are nearly on you, and he opens it, and you get out and you run for it, run, run, run, run down the Fulham Road to the tube station, the streets empty, the cacophony of London hatred emanating like a poison cloud from the stadium, and you don't turn round to see if the lads are following you because you're too busy running and running

Even though you have run like a chicken, you feel the adrenalin, and you feel it ooze and radiate slowly around your body.

You buzz.

You sit on the half-empty tube train heading toward St Pancras station and the safety of home. You did the right thing, you think to yourself. You don't beat yourself up about running. There was no upside. You could not win, and to stay was suicide. Notts was 1-0 up and you'd been there.

You'd attended.

No one could ever take that away from you, no matter what the score.

At St Pancras station, you sit in a café on the platform, drink lemonade and eat crisps, and you watch the people get off and on the trains. You wait until quarter to five, and you stand outside the pub in St Pancras station. You are tall enough to try to get a pint of bitter - some of your friends were already drinking at fifteen - but you've promised your dad you won't. You can see the television above the bar. You can see the result screen. Frank Bough is talking about something. The station is empty, but you know it will be packed before long. You wait for the results to be shown on Final Score. You don't have to wait long.

Chelsea 0 - Notts County 2

Notts County are promoted to Division One.

You clench your fist.

You are ecstatic, but you let no one know, mindful of where you are. Your train is at the platform and you run towards it much faster than you ordinarily would.

Your dad tells you later that Chelsea fans attempted to destroy their own ground after the game, tearing down fences and fighting with the police. A police dog was ripped in half in the Shed. That upset everyone.

A disgrace, everyone said.

Not a police dog. Not an Alsatian. Not a relative of Shep, surely.

Your dad said that he didn't mention any of this to mum because he didn't want to worry her.

He was pleased to see you, you could tell. You tell him that by that time you were on your way home. You don't tell him why.

Chapter 4

The following week, you go upstairs and see Margot in her office. Eunice, her secretary, informs you that she isn't in and won't be in for the rest of the week. She doesn't look you in the eye. This is unusual, and it disconcerts. You try to engage her in conversation, but she's offhand and gives you one-word answers.

You're being frozen out and the process is a slow one, working its way from the top down. Soon, Rupert will stop talking to you. Barbara, the receptionist downstairs. The postman. By the end of it, you'll be talking to yourself just for the company.

That's the way it goes.

In business, in a recession, once you're out, you're out, and there's no way back.

You spend the morning on the Internet, coasting and loafing. You don't *want* to spend the morning on the Internet, and you hardly ever visit normally. You don't do Facebook or Twitter. You don't hang around LinkedIn and the comments section of the Guardian. You're a grafter, and you like it face-to-face. Rupert and John notice but don't say anything. They go out for meetings. You surf the Internet for Notts news. You check your personal e-mails. You send Rita a note. You forward Perry a recommendation for a new computer game called Rage that is supposed to revolutionise first-person shooters.

You read the BBC website. You can't think of a specific reason why you do it, but the next thing you know, you're calling Beanie. He picks up the phone in seconds.

Yo! He's outside somewhere, the sound of traffic and the indistinct sense of static obscures his voice.

How are you, Beanie?

Not three bad, mate. Not three bad. You at wok?

Just about to go out for lunch. Are you in town?

Corals on Upper Parliament Street. Just done a score on a Romford jolly. Four box. Pooch dint get aht. Drifted aht to five to two cheating cockney cunts. No doubt an extra snorker in dog's snap trough.

You have no idea what he's talking about, but you remember. *You remember.*

Fancy a pint? You ask.

Silence on the other end. You don't know whether it's because Beanie has pressed the exit button on his mobile or whether he's walked into a black hole. The whole exchange feels like you're watching two actors on a stage at the Playhouse. *Waiting For Godot. Rosencrantz and Guildenstern.*

Last week, you hadn't thought of Beanie in fifteen years and here you are, asking him whether he wants to go for a drink. You haven't drunk in your lunch hour since the nineties. Since the era of miserable female bosses, drinking at dinner is generally frowned upon and thousands of pubs have shut as a result. If you are caught with alcohol on your breath, Margot will gross misconduct you. For certain. That's the type of flint-hearted woman you suspect her to be. Not like Dave, your old boss. Nevertheless, you feel detached, but strangely contented with your actions.

If you're buying, he responds. The value of my compulsive gambling can go down as well as up, youth.

Even back in the day, the fighting days, you didn't have more than a pound on the Grand National. You can't empathise.

Sure. Same place?

Not sure whether it's two-for-one today, he replies.

I'm not bothered. See you there in ten minutes.

Cheers, buddy.

You left football behind fifteen years ago. You had no choice. You still go to the match, but you sit with the civilians and you go in and out of the Lane stealthily, avoiding all your old acquaintances. You left it behind because it was all over. It wasn't anything dramatic. It wasn't anything epochal.

It. Was. Just. Over.

You had other options.

Rita, for one.

You got married, and before long, you had Perry.

You sold your flat. You took out a mortgage on a house nestled on the border between Carlton and Mapperley, and you've been there ever since. You progressed at work. You mix with suits and people who play Squash at The Park. You mix with people who discuss the state of the Euro and the likelihood of Greek default. The Nottingham Topic printed a photograph of you at the Colwick Hall hotel at the MD's thank you party - champagne glass in hand, dicky bow, the obligatory business-like, self-satisfied narcissistic face.

Rita and you hold regular dinner parties. You generally go to bed early. You've never been comfortable in this world, but it pays the bills and you can do nothing else. You can't do anything practical like the other football lads.

Bash. Crash. Build. Brick. Join. Solder. Plumb. Electric. Hammer.

You wish you could, but you can't. You're useless with tools. You can scarcely program your DVD player. You can't use Excel and as for Access…

You haven't had a conversation with a man who casually uses the word cunt in so long, its usage leaves an uneasy, almost guilty, imprint on your consciousness. Nobody has called you Buddy, either. Not in a long, long time. Nevertheless, you pick up your raincoat and soon you're off, down into the Pit.

Saw Haxford last night, Beanie says.
Did you?
He says hello.
What does he do?

Distribution. He supplies things. I was in Laddies, and he stopped in to have a win treble at Ludlow.

Did it win?

I dunno. He left it. Good lad is Haxford. Remember Fulham?

You nod. You couldn't make Fulham because you had to attend a motivational personal development course in Glasgow that weekend.

We took six tharsand to Craven Cottage.

That was a great season. One of the best ever. Magnificent season. Proud to be a Notts fan.

It woh, Beanie confirms.

The eyes of the grinning gargoyle follow you round the pub, and there is still the draught coming from behind the bookcase. You suppress the desire to get out of your seat, and go and hunt around for the secret button that opens the doorway to Hell. You hear someone come down the stairs to join you in the confined space. Two young Emos.

One in a long black Priest's coat, theatrical paint on his face and a pair of heavy boots inlaid with a thousand metal studs; the other, a teenage girl, in ripped stockings, a high school tartan skirt and Doc Martens.

They look at you with contempt - *straights!* - and sit down on the table opposite.

How did you get started? Beanie asks.

What?

Wi, football and that. All the fun stuff?

I don't know. I can't remember, you reply.

Carlisle, for me. I was only sixteen. Scrapping in them fields behind their stand. We got battered. Tons of em. Clifton Tommy, the Printer, Preece and that. Six onnus. Sheep-shagging Cumbrian wankers.

Nostalgia hits you like a hammer when you hear those names. You still see them, but apart from the odd hello when you bump into them at the ground, you haven't spoken to them for years. You feel yourself getting excited. You are on your second pint. You consider calling Rupert to say you're going home sick. After all, Margot The Terrible could oust you next week, and you'd be in the same position as Beanie. The thought doesn't bother you much.

You decide that's the beer talking.

I guess it was York away, you say.

York?

Yeh. York away. Eighty-seven. I saw bits and bobs before that, but that was the first real day out I had with the lads. Up until that point there'd been bits; Blackburn at home. City. Northampton. Chester. Nothing enormous...

I think I was there. There were two, or three, good York trips. That was a good day out, York. What we got now? Crawley? Fucking Stevenage? Bring back re-election, that's what I say. Top up?

He points to the pint in front of you.

You have a decision to make.

Go back to work, or sit here talking old times, getting hammered. Your car is at work, but you can leave that there - it's an underground car park and safe as the Bank of England. You've no appointments to keep, and its coming up to the quietest time of the year. You haven't been sick since April when you suffered a heavy cold, and you've not had time off for your ongoing stomach illness since February. The two pints have gone down well, and you're pleased to see Beanie.

Yeh. Okay. Another pint, you reply. You take off your tie and loosen your top collar button. Throw in a bag of peanuts, you add, handing Beanie a ten pound note. Get a couple. I'm just going to make a phone call.

You make the phone call outside.

Rupert sympathises with you, tells you that he was only just mentioning to John that you looked peaky that morning. Cheerily, he wishes you a speedy recovery and says see you tomorrow.

You feel instantly guilty. You're not a liar, but this is the whitest of lies and Rupert isn't the target - it's all aimed at the shoulder-padded corporate slapper in the top office. Probably a dyke as well, a vicious man-hating dyke. Beer is amplifying your dislike of Margot, and you spontaneously think malevolent thoughts that come with an intensity you haven't experienced for years.

You spend the rest of the afternoon drinking with Beanie and talking about the old days. Later, in the Magic Spoons on the Square, Beanie introduces you to some of his drinking pals, a mixture of Forest and civilians. Plastics who haven't been to a live football match this millennium. One talks animatedly and in some detail about Man United and later, when he goes to the toilet, Beanie tells you he hasn't seen Man United live since Frank Stapleton.

That's Sky for you.

Football through a lens. Window shopping at Harrods. Internet Porno. Wearing Wellies on the beach.

The gang leave the Spoons behind because it reeks of microwaved food, the beer tastes like dog piss, and it's too quiet because they don't play music. You wish that God would come down on his golden chariot and punish all the Magic Spoons pubs for the parasites they are, but you know they're popular with football lads because they are the only place you can get a cheap session beer, now that they've forced hundreds of other pubs to shut down. Session beers. One of those weak pints you can drink all day and still have enough left about you to get a hard-on for the missus, or to order pie, chips and peas at the chippy. Many pubs today serve overpriced, small brewery high-octane rotgut, which turns you into a swamp donkey after five pints.

The gang find a pub with music on Parliament Street. The Coach and Horses. You stop drinking pints at four and go onto halves because you haven't drunk like this in years and you're talking complete bollocks, just like you used to...

...shitting yourself on the bus home was a waste of time. When you walk through the door, you know that Rita isn't in. You also don't see much evidence of Perry. It's six thirty. You walk into the kitchen.

You see a note on the kitchen table.

At Donna's. Back about ten. I've plated-up a pie. It's in the oven. Bisto in cupboard. Perry's staying at Dan's house. Rita.

You have a friend who works in the music business: Even he appends his text messages to you with an X. Rita's message wipes away the glow of the afternoon's drinking, but at least you think you aren't going to get an earful. You suspect she wouldn't. Your feelings are more like classical conditioning in action, expectancies more than actuality. It's been ages since she raised her emotions enough to berate you for something. You could burgle Laura's house next door, rape her in her own bed, and your beloved wife still wouldn't bat an eyelid when the Rozzers came round to pick you up.

You open the oven door. There is a plate of steak and kidney pie, chips and garden peas on the middle shelf, but you're not hungry. Certainly not for this and even if you were, you can't be bothered to make the gravy. You find a carrier in a drawer, tip the food into the bag, go outside and put it all in the green wheely-bin. You don't feel guilty.

In fact, she's pissed you off. You realise that Rita is drifting away from you. You've been married fifteen years. It happens. You're numb about it. You go to the fridge and take out a can of Stella. The heating's on, and you sit down on the sofa fully clothed. Crack open the beer. You get up and program some music on your laptop resting on the dining room table. You don't know why - well, you *do* know why - but you've had the urge lately to listen to music popular in the late eighties and early nineties. The Stone Roses. Happy Mondays. Primal Scream. Stuff you haven't listened to in years. She may have pissed you off, but at least you can listen to music in your own front room without cans.

Rita is one of those women who see the TV as a constant companion. It's always on, and if it's soap, she's transfixed. Neighbours. Home And Away. Corro. Emmerdale. Benders. Not just soaps. All the stuff, which the BBC passes off as quality drama, but which is actually just relationship television like East Enders, only set in another part of the country and with different actors; things like Sherlock and Waterloo Road. Rita loves those. Most nights, by nine, she's snoring on the sofa, and you spend the evening watching her from your armchair, wondering when it was that you ended the ritual of stroking her feet as she dozed. Most nights, you're in bed before she is, except at the weekends when you stay up late watching films on the satellite channels. You don't even think about TV. Not the pre-watershed bollocks they serve up to keep you sedated and ready to go to work for The Man with a beatific smile on your face.

You've always loved music. When you were young, you had a vinyl record collection that filled six boxes. Everything from Marvin Gaye to the Pistols. You collected around five hundred CDs with pristine transparent cases in mint condition, not a scratch anywhere, but you were forced to digitise them several years ago because Rita said there was no room for them, what with Perry growing up.

You sold them for fifty pence each to a second hand shop on Mansfield Road and put the money towards Laura Ashley wallpaper for the hall and staircase, and a pair of lime-green curtains with a ninety inch drop for Perry's room.

The opening bars of *I Wanna Be Adored* fill the front room, and you take a sip of your beer.

Within minutes, you don't give a shit that your wife is out and that your son hasn't greeted you when you come home from work since he was five.

You suppress an urge to dance around your front room in your suit and raincoat.

York 1987

York City. First match of the season. August 1987.

You see them coming, and at first you think they're York. You're expecting them. You've been told that York hang around the train station before home matches, and you've been on your guard. Leeds play tomorrow, and you expect York to add a few ringers to their ranks. Possibly Boro.

Nasty, Boro. Stab merchants and well known for enjoying a twenty-on-one party. Most hooligans have contempt for Boro. Vultures and jackals.

You've passed through the railway tunnel, and you're walking along the bridge into historic York. The burning August sun hovers in a clear sky. You're glad you're only wearing a tee-shirt, (Kappa, lemon). There are twenty of you, with a further ten up ahead, hunting for a decent pub - beer being the big priority for many Notts.

You know quite a few of the lads from last season, your first season following Notts since you graduated from London University with a degree in History. You have a year left on your Young Person's Railcard, and until you find a decent job, which is proving harder than you thought (and is upsetting your dad something rotten), you've resolved to spend the year following Notts.

Why not? It's your love.

You work full time in a newspaper distribution warehouse. It's tedious, and the people you work with are knobs, but jobs with your kind of qualifications, but no experience profile, are hard to find in Nottingham and you don't fancy moving. Not until the end of this season, at least.

There's about thirty York.

You run the rule over your assembled gang. See what the chances are. Are you going to stand, or are you going to run? Last season was a quiet season with little to write home about.

You had heard rumours that things on the terraces were going to step up a gear, and when you arrived at the station, you were surprised to see the roll call. It looked like a Who's Who, and you suspected that the rumours of a big season on the terraces were true.

Walking along next to you is Clarkson, wearing a green Lacoste polo shirt and trainers. Bulky, hairy, big forearms. Skinhead. He's marching purposefully. He spots the York before you do and he turns. He loves a scrap, latterly being released after three months inside for a nasty little ruck with the Border City Firm in the Cup.

There's Breaker. Fond of a punch-up. Tall, always wears proper gear to the match, which is unusual. Hardly any Notts fans had joined in the sportswear craze. You enjoy all that stuff. You're always in the sports shop. Ellesse. Diadora. Fila. Tacchini. Aquascutum. Lacoste. Nike. You carried on when you were at University, and you could afford it because you had a weekend job in a hotel, earning an extra few quid to supplement your grant. You are always well turned out. You take a pride in your appearance.

Breaker is one of the few - plus some of the Arnold lot - who bother.

The rest of the Notts firm are refugees from Vic Market. Dressing in the dark, colour blind, borrowing whatever they can find from the unsorted back room of a charity shop. Travelling with them can be a trial. Find yourself sitting next to one or two of them on a train, and you often need to hold your nose. Beer fumes, three-day-old underpants, the acrid afterburn of a million fags much more prevalent than a dab of Aramis aftershave.

At the head of the march is Haxford. He's not really a hooligan, and he's a lot older than you are. He organises tickets and coaches and is something of an entrepreneur. You've only ever spoken to him briefly, at Swindon. He is a butcher and along with Crazy Jack, is one of the biggest drinkers on the firm. He can start at eight in the morning, and he'll still be going in the Arriba at two in the morning. You wouldn't even know he was out of it.

Then there's Tom. Clifton Tom. You speak to him on occasion. He's a pisstaker. Always on the lookout for weakness, something he can latch on to.

Nevertheless, he's always cheerful, your size and the early signs of a moustache on his face. He persuaded you to travel to matches on the train late last season.

You notice a strict hierarchy.

Tom will talk to you only when there is no one around he knows better than you. If he knows someone, like Haxford, or Little Dave, or The Printer, he'll shun you like a leper - this kind of male social group being governed by strict social rules. These blokes have been going to matches together since the seventies, and you respect the experience. The rules don't bother you all that much. You're a loner and happiest being alone - just as long as it's in a crowd full of Notts.

There are three on the train from Arnold, but you don't know their names. They don't talk to you. You recognise them, but you went to a different school in the town and you are Catholic. Your two respective schools used to fight. You avoid each other.

You've been going to Notts for ten years and some of the rest are half-familiar to you. The days when like you, they were kids, standing with their dads on the Roadside. One of them works in a bank. Another at John Collier's. Another is a civil servant. Like you, they are mad Notts. They follow Notts, and that's that. When you cut back the bullshit, you are all part of an elite club, and you will never follow anyone else. You speak to these half-strangers when the opportunity arises, but they tend to keep to their own groups of mates. You're all right with that.

You don't complain.

Behind you are the two Bully brothers, walking along with Gordon, the lad who works the buffet cars on trains, Asif, the young Pakistani who idolises the Bullys; and Bacchus, the professional shoplifter from Clifton.

The five of them are a strange sight. They look more like a mass release programme from North Camp: All they need is a roll of string-wrapped clothing under their armpits.

There are two of the brothers. One of them has been talking to you on the train, the older one, in his midtwenties. That was the first time either of them has ever spoken to you. You've overheard people talk about them at Meadow Lane. You've seen them wander around the terraces as if they own the place, usually somewhere near the away supporters. Your dad - who hardly goes to the game now, working seven days a week at the brewery to pay the mortgage on the new house and the loan payments on the new car - warned you to stay away from them, that they were bad sorts.

Even though the influence of your father had naturally waned, his words made you wary. Nobody seems to know their names.

You asked Tom one time, on a train back from QPR.

What are their names?

Who?

The Bullys. What are their first names. Their Christian names.

Dunno, chief. They're just the Bully brothers. I've never asked their names.

Why are they called the Bullys, you ask, curious.

Tom downs the rest of his Stella and points down the carriage where the Bullys were sitting quietly on their own, drinking and smoking, contemplating something. He lights a cigarette and blows the resulting smoke in your face, irritated. Tell you what, youth, why don't you go down there and fucking ask *them*, he says. I'm sure they'll be pleased to tell you.

You didn't bother. For the rest of the journey, you don't talk much, upset that Tom had reared up on you as he was wont to do when drinking.

There is the younger one, younger than you are.

Not even in his twenties yet. Dirty-blonde hair, a neck the size of a kart tyre, built like a centre half, a giant kid, with a crescent-shaped scar underneath his left eye. He's wearing a pink sweatshirt and some strange loafers. Easy Rider sunglasses. Just looking at him makes you uneasy. You can handle Shadies, the sportswear men, the casuals, because generally they don't want to get their Fila tracksuits ripped and torn, but blokes like him who dress like survivors of a nuclear attack, they scare you.

Younger Bully is universally known on the terraces as someone you do not want to upset.

The police know this, and you've heard that they've taken to following him and his brother around the country.

Apparently, they are as popular with the older Notts fans as a leper at a Christmas party carrying a sprig of mistletoe. Once, he ambled past you in the away stand at Doncaster. Someone behind you described him as everything that was wrong with Thatcher's Britain and expressed the opinion that he should be locked up.

A disgrace to football. A fucking hooligan, a good-for-nothing hooligan who gives County a bad name, the older man asserted. Allegedly, he is completely fearless and he's been seen attacking big numbers on his own. He's a walking suicide mission. If you're anywhere near him when it goes off, you're going to be dragged into the battle whether you like it or not.

The Bullys go to every match together. The older one is shorter and bulkier. He has a wedge hair cut, and he's even scruffier than his brother. Today, he's wearing a short-sleeved unbranded charity shop yellow shirt with two big chest pockets for his fags and his sunglasses. Ripped jeans; when he stands, the hem drags on the floor because they are too long for his legs. Scuffed trainers, old-style Nike Bruins, the sole on one separating from the upper. He smokes constantly and is always drunk. He's a complete pisshead. You've noticed that people tend to avoid him. Generally, everyone prefers the younger one. Most people you know consider the older one to be mental, in a lock him up kind of way. His eyes are the weird thing. You can't help but notice him because of his eyes.

You noticed his eyes on the train journey up.

Travelling past Sheffield, for some reason, he started talking to you about horse racing. You have no idea about horses, never having bet in your life, but he seemed to think you were interested. You nodded politely, aware of his reputation as someone who is not quite all there and liable to glass you for no reason in a fit of temper.

He talked about York Races, and you continued to nod politely. Then he leaned forward and starting asking you questions about Notts. You began to think over his endless fag, his relentless can of Stella and everlasting bag of peanuts that he was sizing you up. You don't mind fighting blokes dressed in Tacchini, but you don't want a bloke to batter you who looks as if he's on day release from Rampton.

Luckily, you knew more about Notts then he did and he seemed happy with your answers, even tapping you on the shoulder at one point with a slightly unhinged grin. Disconcerting eyes. They looked into yours, but they weren't really *seeing* you, like eyes on a painting. Painted eyes on an Old Master. Blue when you look at them casually, but look a little closer, and they appear coal black.

Gordon is the tallest of them. You don't know him very well, but he's tight with the Bullys. Same as Bacchus and Asif. Three of the five smoked cigarettes. All through the journey Older Bully and Bacchus chain smoked until the carriage filled with a choking, acrid fog. You noticed a subtle distance between all the groups travelling up on the train - not a concrete distance, there are occasional, casual chats between groups - but subtle separations of time and space. Respecting each group of mates, a loose coalition of which you are no part but your own.

The Bullys spot them first.

Lads! Under the bridge!

There are twenty or thirty of them, equal numbers. From a distance, you suspect that they are older than you, which you don't expect. Thirty-year-olds. There's a bloke at the front who might be as old as your dad. You have enjoyed a couple of cans on the train, but nothing like the quantity of booze everyone else has downed. Notts County have stripped a British Rail canteen clean of canned booze, something they are always doing.

Everyone turns.

You know instinctively that there is no question of running off. The new 1987 season is going to start with a bang. You feel tense and nervous, but you're getting excited.

You want this. You have always wanted this. This is better than anything.

Clarkson says something and you ask him to repeat it. He does.

They aren't York. They're **Newcastle** off to Sheffield.

Newcastle.

A different proposition altogether.

First Division opposition.

Legacy opposition.

You'd be able to talk about this with firms of Legacy teams.

Milwall. West Ham. Stoke. Chelsea.

We had Newcastle at York Station.

The mob stands, and you stand with them.

Newcastle stand under the railway bridge spread across the road. There are equal numbers.

You don't know how Clarkson knows they are Newcastle, but by now, the news has got round.

Newcastle. *Newcastle.*

You are tense and on your toes. You look around, and everyone is grinning from ear-to-ear. The Bully brothers up front, start to run toward the Newcastle lads shouting, Come on, at the top of their voices.

You notice, just before, on the other side of the road, a group of Japanese tourists. They are taking photographs of you and the mob. For a moment, a brief moment, everything is a still life and the Japanese tourists have caught the British Saturday afternoon perfectly.

Young men, between sixteen and thirty. A blurred rainbow of rose pinks, sunburst yellows, and cobalt blues. About to charge another group of men in a blurred rainbow of slate greys, emerald greens and pristine whites. Carrying cans of Stella and smoking cigarette after cigarette. The tourists whisper under their breaths as they take their photos. Hooligan! Hooligan! The moment is pregnant with anticipation, and like the energy in a chunk of neutron-bombarded uranium, a chain reaction occurs in a split second.

Everyone runs, screaming at the top of their voices, along the bridge at midday on a summer afternoon in York, one of the most beautiful cities in the whole of Europe. You run with the pack of wolves toward your prey and you are exhilarated. This is your first real action. The first time you've taken the initiative.

You know that the Newcastle fans would expect you to run - hierarchies! - but you surprise them, and before you know it, you can see them up ahead, fifty yards, forty, thirty.

You're sprinting. There are some fatties who follow Notts, some genuine porkers, and they are sprinting, bending the laws of physics to their will. You're getting closer and closer, and you know you are going to get involved, that you're going to punch someone for the first time over football, engaging in the national tribal pastime, and you clench your fists, and you hear yourself shouting, Come on, COME ON, exhilarated, inflated, nerves on fire.

Amazingly, the Newcastle hooligans turn one-by-one and start to run back to the station.

You cannot believe what you're seeing.

You run faster to get at them, shouting louder and louder, but they are running faster now (you've won) and you're not going to get a chance to hit, and punch, and kick because they are already over the other side of the road and are running back under the viaduct, and the fatter ones in your mob have stopped running, exhausted.

The exhilaration you feel is something close to heaven.

You can hear the Valkyries sing in Valhalla. You stand there, a cool breeze caressing your face, the sound of victory all around you. The sheer joy. You are flushing. Adrenalin courses through you. You feel the beginnings of an erection, but you control it, dampen it down.

The rest of the day is a blur of mayhem, carnage and loutish behaviour taking place in one of the finest places in the United Kingdom.

One of the most historical.

In 1066, King Harold fought and won a battle with an army of invading Danes outside York at Stamford Bridge, just a fortnight before William the Bastard landed at Hastings and thus, changed the course of world history.

If Harold's men hadn't been exhausted following the forced march from York to the South Coast, there might not have been a British Empire.

Maybe even no football.

Notts County beat York City 5-2 giving a scintillating performance in front of the thousand travelling fans.

There are at least five pitch invasions and the lines of police get thicker around the away seats as the match goes on. You watch Haxford and the boys, plus another five hundred Notts take over a pub and drink it dry. The Landlord sent out for more beer, something that always happens when Notts visit a pub. The Notts chants are deafening, but no one wrecks the pub. (The pub is a cathedral for most Notts fans and thus hallowed ground.) You are not much of a drinker, and Tom winds you up for it. Are you a fucking puff or what? He queries, and you are not quite sure whether he's joking or not. To prevent the tide of unpitying insults and to avoid accusations of homosexuality - interminable social death in this outfit - you continually buy pints of the strongest beer possible and leave pints two-thirds full around the pub. On the supporting pillar shelves. On tables full of chanting drinkers. At the bar. In the toilet.

It's expensive, but worth it socially.

After the match, you witness the enormous Clarkson defying the laws of physics by sprinting across the same station bridge - breaking the record for a hundred metres at the same time - in his zeal to get stuck into the York firm who are waiting near the station. You enjoy a runabout with the Bully brothers , confronting a well-dressed posse of York hooligans, a few of whom are carrying brightly coloured golf umbrellas with sharpened nibs. You catch big Hans - a scruffy fat bloke of German extraction, who is a bit of a mong - hiding under a bench as fierce fighting goes off around him.

You watch Haxford drunkenly exhorting snap-happy Japanese tourists to take a photo of Hans snivelling under the bench. They do so. The Japanese love this. Taking photographs of York Minster doesn't compare to live action photomontages of young British men in vividly coloured sportswear knocking bollocks out of each other on a sunny Saturday afternoon.

They'll be talking about this in Yokohama for a month.

Chapter 5

Margot's office.
Four days later.
She's sitting behind her desk in a grey suit jacket and a lemon blouse. You sit opposite. Ash blonde hair tied back in a ponytail that stretches her skin and makes her face look even more severe. She looks every inch the Businesswoman of the Year. Miss Industrious Nottingham 2011. The Nottingham Topic waits. Evening dress and smiles for the camera. Rectangular graphite Dolce and Gabbana spectacles. Tasteful gold sleepers, nothing too ostentatious. No wedding or engagement ring - married to her job. Probably a laminate muncher like quite a few women at the moment. There's a photo of her parents on Dave's huge desk, much tidier and sparser than it used to be. De-cluttered. A tidy desk is a tidy mind. She's one of those women who thrive on responsibility, are positively rejuvenated by it. Her brown eyes seem to look everywhere. She leans on the desk in front of her.

It doesn't seem right to you to see Margot in Dave's office. It definitely doesn't feel right. You wonder how Dave's doing and a childish voice in your head wishes he'd come back.

I've called you in to tell you that I've decided to delay your disciplinary hearing, she says.

You are surprised and a bit shocked. Why? I want to get it out of the way, you reply.

The Company has no choice. The customer is late with the evidence we need.

The Company? Don't you mean you!

She sits back. There is a faint hint of a smirk on her face, but you decide that you might be seeing things.

We need certain evidence to continue.
Evidence?
A customer of yours has made a complaint about something you've said and apparently, he has

documentary and visual evidence to back up his claims. Statements and the TV tapes.

Yet they've not arrived.

Evidence, huh.

Yes.

Margot, do you genuinely believe that, after twenty years, I'm going to behave like this, whatever it is? Do you think anyone is going to believe it? My colleagues out there are scratching their heads. I haven't had a single problem like this in over two decades working here.

I'm not making any assumptions, she says. Your service is an irrelevance. Your prior history is an irrelevance. A complaint is on file, and I have to investigate. It is part of my job as your line manager.

You imagine this is what a poker face looks like. Her eyes remain focused on yours. You realise that her eyes are not brown at all, but as black as those on a shark, and you realise that she's one of those evil women who don't care about anyone but themselves and their own careers. You feel a flash of self-pity, and then you pull yourself together.

When's the new hearing? You ask.

It's suspended. It could be tomorrow, it could be next year. I can't give you a precise date.

It's hanging over me, Margot. How am I supposed to work?

My guess is that your hearing will be in the next month.

The next month.

It will be in the next month. In the meantime, your annual appraisal is due on the sixth of January.

I know. Who's conducting that?

I am.

You laugh nervously.

You feel like a defendant in a courtroom where even the defence solicitor is a prosecutor and the judges have already made their mind up.

That's going to be an accurate appraisal, you say, with a slight tremor. You don't know anything about me.

I have your personnel folder. Moreover, your year's performance figures - your personal benchmarks and achieved outcomes.

My benchmark and outcomes.

Yes. Your benchmarks and outcomes.

Well, Margot, you're going to do an accurate job of appraising me because you have my benchmarks and outcomes.

That's the new appraisal process. You know that.

Nothing else? Not my customer service, the way I relate to customers I've known for years, my timekeeping, and my willingness to walk the extra mile, the way I relate to colleagues...

It's all down to benchmarks and outcomes, she replies. The rest of it, if not irrelevant, is not critical.

I know, Margot. I went to the same training seminar you did. I want Frank Carroll to be part of my appraisal.

You ask for this because you've known Frank for ten years and he is the last person at Head Office who has worked with you. You go back a long way and you know he will ensure you get a fair assessment.

Frank? Why? Margot replies.

Because he's known me longer than you have and I don't trust you to give an accurate appraisal of my skills. You can read outcomes in two ways as you well know. No disrespect intended.

None taken. He's not coming.

I'll see Personnel if I have to.

Margot smiles broadly and leans forward determinedly.

See Personnel! I'm your line manager. Check your staff handbook. Section 5. Para 3. Subsection 2.1. You can ask Frank - or anyone you choose - to *sit in* on your appraisal, but only your *line manager* can appraise you. And that's me.

All this is worse because you know she's right and Personnel will always back up a member of management. Dave told you that.

Frank too. You know Frank would have to turn down the appraisal request. You were shooting blanks. You stand up. You stare at her for the enemy she is.

...shark-eyed corporate schill evil slapper...

Will that be all, Margot?

She softens a little. Not much, but a little. Don't treat me like this. You're being unprofessional. I'm only doing my job. You're making it difficult for me.

Your job, huh. You want me out, and you are here to get me out. You'll find some way of making that stick. I have a wife and a kid, and I've served this company for two decades. You don't care about any of that. I have no chance, and you know it. I'll call Frank myself.

She doesn't respond verbally, just stares at you coldly. You could have read out the weather forecast for all the impact your rant had on her. You walk out of her office. It's eleven forty five. You walk down the corridor steaming and angry, and you hope no one you like walks past you while you are in that state because you won't be able to talk to them.

You stand in the staff canteen and consider making a cup of coffee. You know you cannot win, and that eventually, this posh dyke from Shrewsbury (a shit club if there ever was one, but a great day out, a top place for a riot), is going to make sure you lose your job.

Two decades plus and some narcissistic man-hating career monster with a smart suit and a bad attitude is going to turf you out on your ear.

You clench your fists. You would slap a bloke. You'd take him outside and give him a kicking. You don't like bullies, but you can't do anything to a woman.

How can you defend yourself?

You can't hit her. You can't even shout at her. If you do, you'll never work, and your reputation destroys itself.

Female managers you think, are the ultimate instrument of control, a brilliant idea from the cartels of brilliant billionaire industrialists.

It's simple, really.

A man can *equalise* with a man bully. He can balance things - man-to-man as it were. Square things up. He can *slap* a man bully in the car park after work. Many of the slapped will even respect him for it because men are used to settling differences like that and have been settling such differences since time began.

A man can take a bully outside and give him a kicking and at least half of his work colleagues, family and friends will still talk to him whether he still has a job or not.

Smack a woman, even a savage bully like Margot, and he becomes a pariah instantly.

A one hundred per cent pariah.

No second chances.

Everyone will hate him. He will lose everything.

You realise that Margot has an open goal in front of her, and she isn't going to miss.

You walk over to the mirror above the sink. You look at yourself. You're pale, and you're putting on weight. Bags form under your eyes. Hundreds of tiny red flecks erupt from blue irises.

You're losing your hair.

You pull yourself together and reach for your mobile.

Call Beanie.

He's in town. He tells you that a horse he backed at Fontwell fell at the third with a tenner of his on the nose. You tell him you'll buy the beer.

Without telling your colleagues your plans, you're out the door and into the glacial winds, buffeting the swarming ranks of shoppers in old Nottingham town.

Home Blood

Nineteen eighty-eight and you have been a hooligan at Notts County Football Club for over a year.

You have become friendly with the other lads. In the past year, you have managed to keep the fact that you are a fighting lad away from your dad, although sometimes, you think he suspects. He is now fifty and with rumours that the brewery where he works is about to close, he has other things on his mind. He works so hard, he hasn't been to a game for three years, even the last game of the season he so loved - not even last year's play-offs. Though you love your dad, this state of affairs suits you. His absence allows you to immerse yourself deeper into the culture of violent misbehaviour you have come to adore so much.

You have managed to get yourself an office job in town. It's decent money, and the boss, Dave Farrar, likes you. He's a plastic Man United fan, but you don't mind that. You don't want to work for someone who knows what you get up to at weekends.

That could be tricky.

Your work is boring, but you get out, mostly round places like Norwich, Stowmarket and Ipswich.

Sometimes you find your work and your hobby incongruous.

Sometimes it jars.

One minute you're chasing a firm of Derby down a road in Long Eaton, the next you're discussing unit expansion strategy with a sales director in Felixtowe.

You can't justify it, really.

You should be married, first kid on the way, shopping at Waring and Gillow for furniture on a Saturday afternoon, reading novels to help you sleep, your missus pregnant, concreted with expensive night cream, harping on about her sister's varicose veins. Whiling away Saturday afternoons talking about new cars with your neighbour in a new split-level build on some new greenfield estate.

Instead, here you are, single, pocket full of cash, getting fatter, getting sharper, wearing a steel grey Lyle and Scott V-neck golf pullover that matches today's early winter sky; tight-faded Levis and Adidas Forest Hills with three gold stripes, about to get stuck in to a mob of cockneys taking the piss in the Roadside seats.

They want it alright.

They're praying for it.

If they didn't want it, they wouldn't have sat there.

There's about ten of you, including the Bullys.

Beanie is there. Sparks is with you. One of the nuttiest hooligans ever to grace the terraces at Meadow Lane. You know him from school. Not your school, another school close by. The Mad Postman is there. Apparently, he attacked six Leeds Service Crew on a train and won. This suicide mission was allegedly carried out in revenge for a cup match in the seventies where Leeds hammered the crap out of his dad. You don't know how true this is because you've never spoken to him. He doesn't speak much, except to Sparks and some of the Clifton lot. You like to believe the story because you hate Leeds, like everyone else. He has the same sort of dead eyes as Older Bully. A painted-on gaze that passes right through you.

The match is twenty minutes old. You've all been drinking, and you're not watching the game. You have no idea who is playing for Notts. You're scanning the seats behind you and the away terrace on the Kop. You're hunting different game, and the result of the match is irrelevant.

You've started to drink. You don't know when you started to drink, but you've started to drink as if your initiation into the world of heavy Notts County drinking was inevitable and had always been inevitable. You're not drunk - that will come later, at the Bench and Bar, in the Fountain, the Dog and Bear - but you're immune to thought and feeling, except for snake-brain excitement.

You're standing next to Sparks. He's wearing a huge blue fur-lined coat (which makes you feel warm just to look at it), and black paramilitary boats with a steel toecap. He's lean and gaunt, with sunken cheekbones, sharp blue eyes. He's your size but seems bigger somehow, in line with his legend.

Brentford are in the seats, Sparks says to you.

I can see them, you say.

There's some more in the bogs.

How many in total?

About twelve. Cockney wankers. I hate cockneys.

Cockneys are all right, you reply. You are reminded of your time at UCL, and while Cockneys get on your nerves with their endless boasting, they are nowhere near as irritating as Northerners.

Each to their own. I hope you're in the mood to batter your cockney friends.

I didn't say they were my friends, you laugh. I just prefer them to northerners.

I get on with northerners, Younger Bully says.

Me, too. The Postman says.

There is a full-scale debate about the merits of Cockneys and Northerners.

Somehow, it ends with you and the gang all agreeing on hating Stoke.

While the debate fermented, you recalled a great story about Sparks. One evening, he and his friends were drinking in the White Hart in Arnold, a fun pub on the Mansfield Road. You know it well, one of the best pubs in Nottingham, full of tasty, well dressed girls - a serious chat-up place. People travelled from all over Nottingham. If you kept your nose clean and stayed out of the way, you could sup in there at sixteen and the coppers would turn a blind eye. At least they knew where you were, and you weren't scaring dog walkers by drinking cider in the dark like vampires on freezing benches in public parks.

Chelsea had played Mansfield in the League Cup. Mansfield is fifteen miles north of Arnold, and on the way back a vanload of Chelsea stopped off at the Hart.

These Chelsea weren't families stopping off for a bite to eat at the services - these were handpicked Skins who'd been fighting with Stags outside Field Mill and were still buzzing from the adrenalin. They started hitting drinkers almost immediately, and Sparks got involved. He found himself in the car park surrounded by ten of them - green jackets, Doc Martens, heads like circumcised cock-ends, teeth bared. He was going to die, he knew it.

Instinct and imagination took over. He leapt forward and grabbed the bloke he perceived as the leader, grabbed him round the neck, pulled him away from the pack and backed up against the pub wall. As the rest of the Chelsea came forward, he spun the leader round to face them, put the top third of an index finger inside each half of his mouth and pulled the lips apart so that his gums and teeth were exposed. Boss man yelped and struggled, clearly in some pain. Sparks begins to pull his face apart and said -

If you cunts don't back off and walk back to your van, I'll rip his face off and leave nothing but a grinning skull.

- then tugged his mouth widthways even harder, until the leader started to squeal. His eyes bulged. He gestured to his friends to go away, such was his pain and fear. The Chelsea firm obeyed, walked backwards to the van at the edge of the car park. Got inside.

When he saw this happen, Sparks removed the fingers from Boss Man's mouth, span him round and headbutted him on the nose, leaving him bleeding and dazed on the floor. Ran back into the pub and bolted the door.

Luckily, the police arrived. Rather than arrest the Chelsea mob, they picked up the stricken leader, put him back in the van and escorted them out of Arnold, and up Oxclose Lane to the M1. Sparks is too cool to tell this story about himself, but it is legend around Arnold.

You know that Brentford's lads have spotted you. Talking among themselves. They are the same age, early-to-mid twenties, and dressed to the nines in high-quality gear, some of it you don't recognise. Your two groups are in accord. Neither group shouts or yawps because neither group wants the attention. They don't cheer when Brentford's striker sends a screamer onto the crossbar. The filth are absent today for some reason, and what coppers there are, congregate on the away terrace. Older Bully reports that there isn't a single copper in the Roadside. Asif, who tends to follow him energetically, being only sixteen, confirms this, but Sparks doesn't listen to him and refers to Older Bully as the rules suggest. Very few people get to talk to Sparks. He picks and chooses who he talks to, being right at the peak of the hierarchy.

There are some other blokes hanging round.

Sparks' pals, Culvert and Church.

Whisky Jack and Godfrey, who are both from Newark. They love fighting with a passion you can bottle and sell. With those lads, your mob and Brentford have even numbers; a balance. The rest of the lads are over in the Main Stand. You're glad. You don't want any more with you, otherwise, the coppers will come from all over and stop the ruck before it starts. You don't want a riot this afternoon. You want a *scrap*. A nice ten versus ten would clear the winter cobwebs nicely, thank you very much.

The plan is to take them at half time by the coffee hatches underneath the stand. Brentford know that.

The match, like most involving the team you love, is tedious, and you cannot wait for the half time whistle. Football itself is like war. Ninety percent boredom and ten per cent pandemonium. As the moment approaches, you feel the tingle. Adrenalin starts to mount, and it is all you can do to remain cool. You really want to jump around like an Alpha-orang-utan about to face a challenger for the females in the harem. The energy inside you is a chain reaction waiting to happen. You look round, and you sense that you all feel the same.

Everyone is smirking, naughty kids about to do something especially naughty, the collective grin of the insane.

Violence. Football violence.

Ultra Violence.

Nothing can beat it.

The whistle goes for half time, and you're straight downstairs behind the Bully brothers. Sparks walks behind you. He doesn't do anything quickly. He sort of *ambles.* You see the Brentford getting out of their seats as one. You group. You wait at the bottom, all ten of you, bouncing, bouncing, (c'mon, c'mon, c'MON) and you wait for all the tea drinkers and dads and kids to dissipate, and you see them, the Cockneys, but you do a double take and there's only two or three of them coming down the stairs, they aren't all there and you realise that you've been blindsided, and suddenly, you hear them to your right - C'mon you faccin Northern cants! - and startled, you are battered in the side of the head by a bloke wearing a strawberry-coloured Ellesse tracksuit top because they've come down the other steps on the other side of the coffee bar, and you've been outsmarted, and you turn round to defend yourself, and he hits you, a decent, hefty punch, and you feel your nose go, and your legs, and before you know it, you're on the floor.

All hell lets loose.

You look round from below. Older Bully slaps a lad in a yellow Fila jacket under the terrace supports. Godfrey throws a cup of tea in the direction of a face, but most of it misses. All the civilians scatter, the dads, the pensioners, the kids, the few women who come down

Notts, and suddenly, there is a big empty romper space for the boys to play in. A Brentford lad attempts to kick you in the face with a Nike Leader trainer (with the red stripe). Instead, it connects with your neck, and you roll over, watch Sparks wade into your assailant, a ghostly blur of spectral darkness, chunky blue coat, a wraith. You watch him throw a steamer, his arm extending in slow motion, like the cracking of a whip and you see it connect with your assailant's chin. You get up off the floor. You should really kick him back, and kick him, and kick him, but you leave it because you remember, you *remember*. You watch Whisky Jack jump on a tall cockney in a Tacchini kagoule and Aquascutum jeans, and they go straight down in a heap. Younger Bully has another in a headlock, trying to bash his head on a wooden strut. Asif has two Brentford round him, a common problem (with him being Asian), two stick one, three stick one, and they're kicking seven bells out of him. You jump over to help, lamping one of them in the side of the head, booting the other, and Asif gets up and kicks out wildly, at random, an ear-piercing shout on his lips.

Just when things are getting interesting, flashes of yellow appear from nowhere - coppers - and Sparks taps you on the shoulder. Instinctively, you back away, mingle with the civilians; *merge* like drops of fragmented mercury into one coagulated mass. The Notts crowd are pissed off with Brentford - well, mostly. Someone kicks you on the thigh, but you cannot tell who it is. Someone else calls you a wanker, and an old boy wearing horn-rimmed glasses, which make him look like Peter Sellers, calls you a fucking hooligan.

The crowd opens up like the Red Sea and lets you down toward the home end. There's just you, Sparks and Asif, and you don't look back to see who else has escaped and who is destined for a long bleak night in the basement cells at Central Station. Nobody wants to spend too long at Central. Nobody with a sense of smell, at least.

After the match, you regroup. Godfrey and Whisky Jack are waiting for you outside. The Bully brothers. Sparks. Some others join who weren't there at half time. There have been no arrests, but several Notts and Brentford were ejected, including the pair of Newark lads.

You've lost touch with the Brentford firm, and you walk up County Road. Most Brentford leaving the ground came on coaches, but as you pass them, you suspect the ten in the seats are travelling on the train. You guess right. You spot them on London Road up ahead, and you begin to trot after them. They see you, and they trot away up the canal toward the station. You run, but you never quite catch them - always, like a dream, one tantalising step ahead.

As you arrive at Nottingham station, they're surrounded by coppers on the station concourse, waving at you cheerfully and giving you the wanker sign. Inviting you down to Griffin Park for a rematch.

You laugh. The game is over. It is incumbent upon you to go down to London and return the compliment. You can't wait.

Chapter 6

By the time you get home, Rita is fast asleep on the sofa. She doesn't even hear you come in. East Enders is on. She snores lightly. She hasn't cooked anything for tea.

After meeting Beanie at dinner, you went back to work in the afternoon, but returned to the pub after work.

It seemed that in the interim, Beanie had been busy. Some old faces from Notts arrived, and they greeted you like an old friend with hugs and backslaps. Clifton Tom appeared, and within seconds, he was ripping the piss out of you. Unmercifully. The Printer appeared, and he was punching and kicking you on the shoulders and arms, play fighting, offering you outside, just as he used to. Little Dave popped in for a Pils and greeted you like a long lost brother.

Preece arrived. He worked at a famous bike maker, a time served toolmaker. He now works for an agency on a production line because the historic bike maker moved to a freshly deforested industrial zone in Indonesia where imprisoned children make the bikes for twenty-eight pence an hour and the western reps spend their bonuses on sex with their mothers.

Preece's experience made you think.

You know that you are never going to get another job when Margot successfully does what fifty football firms around the country failed to do.

You might be bright, but you're also old.

You're past it.

You're old school.

You're not brilliant on a PC. You use first names and shake hands, and the kids don't do that. They call you mate and you have seldom called anyone mate in your life. Australian influence. Mate. They even talk to clients like that and strangely, don't lose business. You have to suppress the urge to tell many, many young people you know that you are *not* their mate, but you know it would be pointless saying anything, so you don't. You're old-fashioned and very expensive. Twice the price of a twenty-five-year-old with a two-two in Business Studies from one of the old Polys. You don't watch X-Factor, you hate rap music, dubstep and all that, and you never watch Match of the Day. You have several spent criminal records and every employer wants an enhanced CRB check to check for imaginary Nonces. Not a normal one, but an *enhanced* one that will highlight your spent convictions. You're putting weight on in direct proportion to your funereal metabolism. You do strange gurning exercises with your jawline to rid yourself of your inflating jowls. You might have liked wearing the casual gear when you were a kid, but that was an affectation, which ended when you got married and Rita got pregnant. You don't moisturise, wax, or depilate. You don't spend eighty quid a month on gym membership. You don't buy designer socks and boxer shorts, or spend thirty seven quid every fortnight at Spikey Mikeys for a just-out-of-bed style haircut - unlike all the shaved and moisturised, douched and perfumed gender hybrid, metrosexual, transmetropolitan, New York worshippers you're about to compete with in the job market.

Gay men scare you.
Black men scare you.
Women scare you.
You're old school.
A historical anachronism.
You're a Warner Pathe newsreel, living your life in black and white.

The world is a different one than the one you fought in, and they may as well hand you the rejection letter before you fill in the application form.

You and the boys in the pub talked about football. The old days. For some reason, you thought deeply about Brentford at home and even better, Brentford away.

Clarkson, who also turned up, talked to you at length about Oxford away, but you don't remember it because you were at a wedding. One of the biggest fights in Notts history and you were at a wedding.

And the happy couple divorced two years later.

You drank six pints and made your excuses. Beanie hugged you, drunk. He told you he loved you, and it made you feel temporarily uncomfortable, but you knew it was just affectionate fun and nothing about to lead to Chutney Junction.

He said it was great to see you. You were mildly aware of something - a descent, the smell of flowers strong and pungent, something behind the door, the draught, a mixture of things - and you said you'd be in touch.

The bus was busy even at seven. Full of shoppers and workers, and students and drinkers. You had to stand and twice, you nearly fell. A woman who looked like Jennifer Aniston's older sister looked at you with contempt.

You've been getting the bus to work whenever you don't have appointments, which is a lot lately, being Christmas. You've been drinking every night for the past seven work nights. You've taken to having a pint or two after work. Sometimes with work colleagues. Sometimes with Beanie and the lads. Just one, or two. Just to unwind. Besides, you suspect Rita doesn't give a shit whether you come home or not, and you *definitely* know that Perry only ever appears when he wants something. You look at Rita while she sleeps on the sofa. Childlike, curled up in a ball.

She's wearing a pink vest and a blue denim skirt, and she's still as beautiful as she was when you first met her. She's wearing fluffy sky-blue socks - the same blue colour as the 2006 away strip - to keep her feet warm.

In the summer, she's usually barefoot. You love to watch her legs and feet. You love to stroke them. You always did. You're still attracted to her as much as you were, and you feel an erection coming on, but you know it's pointless. You haven't had sex in three months, and even then she wasn't really all there.

Emotionally, she's pulled away from you, a brother and sister situation where sex feels like incest, when it feels like anything at all, and when Perry reaches eighteen and University, she'll be off.

She's only just forty. She's still young enough to pull and still gets admiring glances. You've seen your neighbour: He can't take his eyes off her. She's more or less told you that she's a divorce waiting to happen. Not in so many words, but you know. You *know*. You want to go over there to the sofa and touch her. Hold her. Stroke her arms and shoulders, remove her socks, and draw tiny imaginary pictures with your fingertip on her varnished toenails. Curl up with her, mould your body into her back so the pair of you are seamless, a whole, not knowing where she begins and you end, the perfect marriage, but you know that if you do, she'll tell you to fuck off and elbow you in the face.

The thought makes you feel unbearably sad.

You get up and go upstairs to see Perry. You knock on his door. You open it and say hi. Perry turns round from his Call of Duty game and waves you away dismissively, tells you he's talking to someone.

He tells you to shut the door on your way out.

Bereft, numb, you go to your room and you lie on your bed in the darkness, staring at light patterns cast by the streetlights on the ceiling.

The Sixth Circle

December 10th. Nineteen Eighty Eight. FA Cup Second Round. Hartlepool United Away.

Notts had beaten Darlington in the first round, and this was the reward. You are sitting on a shuttle, edging slowly toward Hartlepool, and you are not going to have time for a pint before the match. None of you are happy about that. A delay between Langley Mill and Alfreton cost nearly an hour. The buffet car from Sheffield to York was shut with no reason given, and none of you had the foresight to bring a supply of beer. You're all thirsty enough to drink a barrel of lager. Each.

There are just six of you on the train. You're with the Bully brothers, Asif, Bacchus and Gordon. You expected a bigger turnout for this cup match, but most of the lads are travelling up in cars.

The Bully brothers are in a bad mood and have been niggling at each other since Leeds. They are both in need of drink. Older Bully suspects a conspiracy by the British Rail management to stop alcohol sales in order to quell endemic football violence. Younger Bully, evidently more sensible in matters like this, disagrees.

You look across at Gordon smoking and staring out of the window. Tall, fair haired, skinny when compared to the usual girth of the Notts fan, almost wiry. He is the type of man who smiles a lot, the result of someone dropping him on his head as a child. He's laid back, never seems to have an axe to grind; he makes for an unlikely football hooligan.

Last year, Younger Bully and he staged a two-man raid on Bristol City's executive seats. They took a serious kicking - as they would, with Bristol City a legacy firm - and afterwards, they had to sprint all the way from Ashton Gate to Temple Meads while being chased by fifteen City bent on revenge.

In the weeks afterward, they were lauded for their cheeky bravery. Gordon, typically modest, told people who asked that the pair of them went in that end by accident. No one believes a word.

He dresses in dark blue or black, standard, nondescript shirts and jeans, like a male version of Siouxie, out of the Banshees.

He is trying to calm the situation down. He tells them that sometimes Inter-City trains are short staffed. That was probably the issue. And he should know, seeing as he works for British Rail catering.

The resemblance comes to you in a flash. Older Bully looks like Shaun Ryder of the Happy Mondays, only fatter. The same nose, the same pudgy cheeks, the same pudding-basin haircut. He isn't happy. His eyes are more like black holes than usual, deep trenches underneath, coal bunkers and his essence is a strong mix of frustration and annoyance. Everyone round him experiences this. It is difficult to sit next to him without gagging as you did on the train before this one because he has been smoking non-stop since Nottingham, and he had clearly been on the beer the night before. A heavy session. Suspended in the upper echelons of the carriage is a Whitechapel smog, most of it due to his and Gordon's constant Benson and Hedges. You have never smoked and have never had any inclination to do so. Asif sits quietly, a gentle grin of wonder on his face, tapping his fingers on his blue jeans in some rhythm known only to him. He's a strange one. Most of the lads in the cars can't be doing with him, and you suspect it's a racist thing. Notts aren't a liberal club and Nottingham isn't a liberal city. The Bully brothers have one hierarchical rule: If you're Notts, you're alright. Black, pink, blue, brown. Notts and they'll be seen with you. You do wonder whether he is the only Muslim football hooligan in the country. You don't know for sure. There must be others. He's only just left school, and he hasn't a blemish or scar on his face. He's at college studying art. Eyes like something from a Manga comic. He looks a bit like Michael Jackson circa *Thriller*.

Bacchus sits quietly opposite you reading the sports pages of *The Sun*. He landed a major score yesterday, raiding Wardrobe and coming away with two Armani sweaters, a pair of two hundred quid loafers and five high-quality belts. He sold them for half price out of the bag last night in the Dog and Bear to a gang of Forest on a birthday crawl. Wardrobe is only small, compact and bijou, right next to The Fountain. Catering for the Park set.

No prices displayed. If you have to ask the price of an item in Wardrobe, you can't afford it.

Wardrobe and Limeys are the only suppliers of proper suits in the East Midlands and gentlemen with an inclination toward high-end fashion come from all over the Midlands to buy. Naturally, every Clifton shoplifter worth his salt targets the place despite heavy security. The shop has bouncers. You wouldn't think it was possible to rob Wardrobe, a Fort Knox equivalent, but Bacchus swears he had it off. With a special carrier bag, apparently. He tells you that he and another lad from Cotgrave invented the carrier bag lined with metal foil to stop detectors from spotting stolen goods. You don't believe him and neither do the Bullys, but he swears it is true. He opened his wallet earlier and he was carrying more than the rest of us combined. He has never worked a day in his life, being a professional front-of-house scam artist, robber of shops, and plastic card fraudsmith. That was all he ever wanted to be.

You try to imagine the final fifth year interview with his careers teacher - until you remember that there aren't any careers teachers in Clifton.

Most of the money he earns goes in slot machines, on drink, or following Notts, or some combination of the three. Earlier, he confessed to being an ex-alcoholic.

During his last stretch in Lincoln, eighteen months for passing stolen cheques, he volunteered for an Antibuse plus Counselling programme to help him kick the habit. Lincoln at the time, he said, was straining at the seams with grog; slops, hooch and smuggled moonshine distilled in plastic bins. Yet he swears he didn't touch a drop for his entire stay, but he soon recanted when he got out.

This time, he assured us, he was taking it steady.

Just a couple of pints before the match to liven things up a bit. Just the two.

A couple after the match back at The Fountain to be sociable.

Home early to the missus and kids.

He is the only Notts fan who sports a beard - he looks a little like a young David Bellamy. Two of his front teeth are missing. Like Older Bully, who gets on best with him, there is something odd about his eyes. They look in two directions when he speaks to you.

Earlier on, between Chesterfield and Sheffield, the five of you talked fighting.

Expecting much today, Asif asked no one in particular.

Definitely, younger Bully contributed. Just like Darlo.

Though you weren't there, you were aware there was trouble at Darlington. Notts came out comfortably ahead.

They'll be up for it today, Older Bully commented, drawing deeply on yet another cigarette. They're probably waiting at the station.

Don't think so. It will be too late by the time we get there, Gordon offered. They'll kick off after the match, win or lose. Jump us on the way back. I know some Derby lads who took a pasting up here. Horrible place, Hartlepool. Nothing to do but sup, fuck, nosh and batter lads like us.

I'm not worried, Older Bully said. We'll have the Northern cunts.

Less of the Northern, said Younger Bully, still narked with his brother for some reason and mindful of plenty of Northern-based friends.

Piss off, his elder brother retorted. We'll have to get a taxi to the ground otherwise, we're going to miss the kick off. Do they have taxis up in this shithole that carry five?

Do they have taxis up here? Asif asked, ironically.

You'd know, said Younger Bully, wryly.

What about a pint? Bacchus interrupted.

Older Bully shook his head. I've heard there's nothing round the station, he replied, an air of disappointment. I'm fucking desperate for one, but there's nothing in Hartlepool but druggies, fucked monkeys and kiddy fiddlers. We may as well go straight to the game and wait for afters back in civilisation.

Bacchus looked disappointed. That's a pity. I could murder a pint. Settle me willies.

Not scared by any chance, my friend? Older Bully asked slyly.

Nah, not me. Like a swift half before the match, that's all.

Hartlepool is one of the most deprived areas in the whole country. Thatcher had done a number on the main industries - the steel, the shipping, the docks and the coal. Nothing left up here. Zero. A scorched earth policy passed by a southern elite who fly straight past. More women than men work in Hartlepool, in part time jobs on the High Street, or in the corner shop. Fifty per cent unemployment, a hundred per cent hopelessness and the locals are angry about it. Visiting football supporters tend to be the outlets for that anger.

Especially Southerners - a relative category in which visitors from Nottingham nestle snugly.

You look out the window as the train rolls into the town, a smell of sulphur stirred by the old train's brake. The hellish smell matches what you see outside. The

North Sea, a dank, restless, murky, overfished, oil-slicked and polluted stretch of water on the edge of Europe. In the silver grey sky, a flock of seagulls escapes inland, a storm brewing out in the mist. A post-apocalyptic tableau, as if someone had exploded a thermonuclear device nearby - a Doomsday weapon that had demolished everything for twenty miles. The few remaining Satanic Mills now ruins, ghosts, stark mausoleums, the foundations on which they stand fragile, the soil poisoned and infertile. It is getting dark outside. An inkling of snow in the air and a gathering wind. You spot a gaggle of dirty kids digging for something, perhaps buried treasure, atop a heap of chemically enhanced soil and rocky debris. Others cycle up and down toxic hillocks on Choppers and Grifters.

The train trundles into an outer district; row upon row of terracing. Kerbsides stripped of their cars, streetlights yet to flicker. Behind that, in the distance, you see more dead grass, more slag heaps crawling with hopelessness, gravel and rubble. You pass malformed metal shapes, strange unidentifiable wreckage and blasted brickwork. More rocks, miles of coiled wire, torched vans and burned out cars - the desolate inheritance of a proud industrial past, gutted and filleted for no real reason other than the vengeance of a shopkeeper's daughter.

You are uneasy.

This kind of environment creates monsters, and you are not expecting a result. The only result you really want is to get in, watch Notts get through to the third round and a potential moneyspinner with a proper club - a City, a Liverpool, a United, maybe even Forest - and get out of there as fast as possible.

You've had a good season so far with several good rucks around the country. You're making a name for yourself as someone who can be relied upon in a punch-up. You don't cry, and you don't run. If you're taking a kicking - like that time in the car park at Walsall, or at Doncaster station with Palace - you take your beating like a man.

You've been invited today by Younger Bully, and you had to come whether you wanted to or not. There was no choice. You're no shitter, but you'd much rather be watching the Lumberjack Championships this afternoon than trying to survive this hellhole.

You tell no one this for obvious reasons.

The announcer tells you that you are approaching Hartlepool, and you stand, you all stand, walk to the doors. Gordon is right. You don't expect to see Hartlepool because they'll assume you are already at the match. There's hardly anyone at the station as the train pulls in and you almost leap off onto the empty platform. At a trot, you walk up to the front. Bacchus notices a buffet, and it's open. There is a short debate, and it is decided to buy a quick can each to steady nerves.

Bacchus pays for five cans of cold and overpriced Stella. On the taxi rank, the five of you stand in a circle like musketeers, and salute each other and the mighty Magpies by clinking the cans together. You down the beer in one gulp and together, the five of you throw the cans into a bin with a loud clatter.

Older Bully negotiates with a taxi driver to carry five to the ground. The driver shakes his head - four only - but Younger Bully pulls out a tenner, and that twists his arm. It's a quiet afternoon, and the driver can't afford to turn down business. You get in the taxi with the leviathan Younger Bully in the front seat. It's a squeeze, but having Asif with you, who is tiny, helps ameliorate the crush. You're all laughing; the single can of beer enough to lift the tension. The driver pulls out into the traffic, and you're on your way into Hell -

-that's the only way you can describe the scenario that unfurls in front of you like a bad horror film, bad in the sense of scary, rather than crap - a *Psycho, a Night of The Living Dead,* a *Blood on Satan's Claw,* an *Evil Dead,* Dead, Dead, Dead, the Dead Walking.

There are three hundred lads below the away seats, and they're baying for your blood.

Somehow, your little posse has been split up, and you and Older Bully are in the seats with forty Notts while the others are trapped with the thousand fenced in on the other side of the death-trap ground. This is by some way the worst ground you've ever been to, a condemned firetrap, a danger to everyone; decomposing stands, seemingly made from the reclaimed wreckage of ocean going dredgers, rotting planks for seats, exposed nail heads protruding like steel mushrooms from the joists ripping into your thighs.

In the seats, are a mixture of civilians and hooligans, the usual gang, Breaker, Clarkson, Tom, The Printer, Little Dave, Haxford, more of them, but they're not as loud as usual, nowhere near as arrogant, because on the terraces below, separated by a six foot drop, and a disintegrating wooden partition painted royal blue, are the baying Hartlepool lads.

Rorke's Drift in the North East.

Not dads, or sons, or cloth-capped locals with a pie and a rattle, not old soldiers in Crombies, nor sailors in woolly hats, but lads, lads, lads everywhere and they aren't looking at the game, the rather sterile episode of cup football on the pitch; they glare in your direction, and they try to climb up the partition, and you rack your brains to remember when you have last seen such loathing on human faces.

You hear Clarkson say that they aren't just Hartlepool, but Boro, but you're not interested in the distinction, they're just crazed zombies, shambling, and roaring, and screaming with frozen shark eyes. An ugly one with a strange, pig-like nose and two giant ears manages to get to the top of the partition, but a man sitting in front of you gets out of his seat and pushes him back down. Breaker tells you that the men in front of you are undercover coppers, the only police presence inside the ground because this is ostensibly a Steward Only game, designated as unlikely to be a focus for hooligan activity and the hard-up Hartlepool Chairman won't pay for coppers unless he has to.

Plod are expensive, and times are hard. You only have to look round the Hiroshima-like bombsite that is Hartlepool to understand that. You saw a vanload of coppers outside on your way in. Fat lot of good they're doing out there. Ordinarily, you have no time for coppers after some of the antics you witnessed last season - the battering of Notts fans at Chesterfield for one, over the top police brutality at its extreme - but on this occasion, you wished they'd make an appearance.

You are aware at this point that this is hypocrisy at its most fundamental.

Breaker and Tom tell you that they went to the nearest pub before the game and were driven out by Monkeys, several punches being thrown, and a couple of minor Notts figures threatened with pool cues and broken bottles of brown ale. Some of the real ale beardy weirdies, diehard Notts and intense followers of the Hop, were threatened in the car park. Someone from the back shouts that the Evening Post Weatherman, a fanatic Notts fan, had been punched in the back of the head. Rumours that a bespectacled shirter had been stabbed outside a chip shop circulate, but no one can confirm it.

You're not happy about that. Beating up shirters is like beating up women or kids. Happy clappy non-combatants, generally - programme collectors, statisticians and Shoot readers. A football shirt is a sign of neutrality and disinterest. You don't beat up shirters, never mind stab them. That's an unwritten code. The monkeys had broken a taboo.

You stand up. You're dressed in decent gear - your Lyle and Scott, Nikes and a new pair of Armani jeans - and they've spotted you. In the middle of the baying mob, two young lads point you out and make the universally recognised symbol for throat cutting. You give them the wanker sign back. You notice that there is a fence to their right. That means that they are penned in. They cannot get into the toilet area behind the stand you're sitting in. There is another fence between the stand and the pitch, stopping anyone jumping onto the pitch and circumventing the perimeter fence. They are sealed in.

The horde below - now singing the **You're Going To Get Your Fucking Heads Kicked In** song, a pleasant ditty made all the more joyous when sung tunelessly by a choir of psychopaths - would definitely have invaded the pitch to get at their target, given the chance. Because of the fencing, you work out that you can get tea and a pie at half time. Hartlepool go a goal up and the mob below go mental animal crazy. Several Monkeys powered by adrenalin and the scent of victory, reach the top of the partition and try to get over, but the longhaired copper, who looks more like a country singer, a Kris Kristofferson type, with matted hair and a moustache as thick as rope, pushes anyone who gets to the top back into the pit. You don't feel anything and rather than being upset at being a goal down, or thrilled at the upcoming prospect of a fight back, you start to wonder how you are going to get back to the train station alive.

Some of the "lads" below are in their forties and fifties. Veterans of the carving knife and butcher boy days. The machete shuffle and the lump hammer tango. You spot one bloke older than your dad, and he is apoplectic with rage. Demented, he's banging his forehead on the royal blue partition, cheeks crimson red through too much ale, and flaming eyes agog with irritation. You know that if he caught you outside, he would kick you down, and he wouldn't stop stamping you on the head until you were dead. Men of similar inclination surround him. You assess your chances of making the station alive as zero per cent.

You wonder how it came to this. Saturday afternoon entertainment for the working man.

When you were a kid, you sneaked into a film called *Rollerball*, an AA film. You were thirteen, a year illegal.

Any student of film will tell you that *Rollerball* is one of the worst films ever made, but its concept is robust and clever, repeated several times in the interim. The world is dying, a polluted shell and the population of elites is entertained by the eponymous televised ball game played by gladiators, a game in which participants are burned, maimed and eventually killed in the name of sport. A bit like this visit to Hartlepool.

Look, there's our kid, Older Bully says, tapping you on the shoulder seemingly unconcerned at the scene below him. He's pointing over to the away pen, fenced on all four sides. Younger Bully is being wrestled to the ground by three stewards.

He's trying to get over here, look. That's just like him. He doesn't want to miss the action. That's our kid, hey! That's our kid!

There's Bacchus, look. Tom points out. He looks like Captain fucking Pugwash.

Bacchus is arguing with the chief steward. So is Gordon, more indistinct. There is space around them as the Notts civilians back away from the skirmish. Younger Bully is back on his feet, and the stewards push him into the crowd away from the gate. The stewards are not going to let them through to the seats. They are lucky, but they won't see it like that. They'll see it as missing out. Anyone not in those seats will, the Lion's Den.

The half time whistle goes. Kris Kristofferson in front of us says in a Yorkshire accent that we'll be alright to get a drink and a piss because the away seats are fenced in. You look down below. Hartlepool's lunatics are trying to pull down the fence while the stewards watch.

You wonder whether to stay where you are, but you need a leak. You take the risk, following the rest of them in a line down the rickety back stairs, a fire escape-style egress seemingly pinned onto the stand with sticky back plastic. You are not surprised to find a splinter in your backside, which you quickly remove.

Leaving the sanctuary of the away seats was a mistake and you know it straight away.

You take a quick leak and then queue up in the tea line. The area fills with Hartlepool from further up the stand. Before you even have a chance to order your pie and tea, you are pummelled in the back of the head. *County bastard! Come on then!* You back off. He's in his fifties, and he's pissed out of his head. It feels like being attacked by one of your dad's mates from the brewery. Another old boy in glasses, who looks like he should be delivering bottled milk from a van at six in the morning, kicks you hard in the back. You back off further down toward the pitch. Up ahead, you see Little Dave go down surrounded by six blokes twice his age. Tom is fighting for his life with four younger lads in sports gear. Breaker and Clarkson are under pressure by the exit door, eight stick two. The rest of the Notts are running back to the seats, amidst a torrent of fists and boots. You switch into panic mode and slap the milkman, knocking off his glasses, which enrages the fenced-in animals to your side. You connect beautifully, flooring him, but you resist the temptation to frame the moment because the other old boy has punched you in the side of the face, a stinging punch. You run backward, instinctively. Older Bully throws a boiling cup of tea in a face, and you hear his victim scream. You watch him kick the man in the face and he goes down holding his head for two separate reasons. He gestures to you to run with him. You swing at the old bloke who hit you first (a hefty left, which smarts and bites), but you miss, and he laughs at your pathetic effort. He ignores you and punches Older Bully, who hits him back with an absolute beauty, knocking him over and making his nose gush. You push another old man away, and the two of you run back toward the steps. There is no way you can save Little Dave who is being hammered to shit by six blokes, stamping him and grinding him into the toilet wall. By contrast, you receive several more punches and kicks, not especially good ones, and you think someone has tried to slash you, but you cannot be sure, the elusive swoosh of something sharp and metal passing your ear like a cool breeze, and you're glad most of these Monkeys are just near-dead old alcoholics, deadbeats, tourists, part-timers, not proper lads, like the ones fenced in round the corner. You'd all be dead if they were. You notice that Little Dave has been picked up by two stewards. He holds his head, cut and bleeding. Older Bully finds himself fighting for his life, retreating up the staircase while being slapped by two lads in proper trainers and sports gear who have appeared from nowhere. One is hitting him on the side of the head repeatedly, and the other is stabbing him in the arm with a dart. You attempt to assist, land a punch, but these are rock-hard lads and your attempt doesn't register, and when it does, a hammer-like right lands square on your nose and you fall down three steps twisting your ankle, but you don't go down, which would be fatal, and the undercover coppers are suddenly round you (thank God), one of them kicking and slapping their northern countrymen every bit as viciously as a thug would. They form a barrier between Hartlepool's lads and yourselves and somehow, miraculously, all the Notts find their way back into the seats.

Older Bully has had enough.

In an ocean blue Fruit Of The Loom jumper, which was in fashion sometime in the late seventies, and with a swaying beer gut, the jumper struggles to contain, he stands up, runs down to the front and starts trying to land blows on the psychos below, the alpha male suicide impulse taking over and he roars, his arms outstretched, chest out, standing proud, unable to control himself.

C'MON YOU FUCKING NORTHERN CUNTS!
COUNTY!
COUNTY!
COUNTY!

Everyone behind him, including you, joins in the chant, an electric feeling, a major adrenalin rush, and you chant at the top of your voice with your arms in the air. This act of defiance enrages Hartlepool and some desperately struggle to climb up the fragile blue-painted partition.

Suddenly, to the left of you, a Monkeyhanger is in the seats, a skinhead with a slash down his left cheek, a blue denim jacket ruined by bleach stains. He gestures with his outstretched hands for you to come and get some, and you are all on him before he can throw a right, and he's booted and slapped, you landing a purler on his left eye socket before he jumps back over the partition into the horde. He gets a round of applause, pats on the back from his mates, and gives the Notts a wanker sign, pogoing like one of the Sex Pistols. The undercover coppers return, surround Older Bully, and tell him to sit down or he's nicked. He does so with a snarl. His face is flushed, and he's going to have a shiner in the morning, a bad one, and he holds his arm where the dart stabbed him, but it isn't bleeding and his damage is nothing compared to Little Dave, who has been stamped on, and had his head crushed up to a brick toilet wall. He stinks of urine because Hartlepool people generally piss on the outside of the concrete toilets and he had been kicked around atop the fresh slush. He's not happy about it, though as the match continues, and discussions start amidst the chaos, which now seems humdrum and every day, the consensus is that Dave is lucky to escape intact. Tom, ever sympathetic, moans that he's going to have to sit next to his piss-stained pal in the car on the way back. He wished, he said with a grin on his face, that he had been fucking hospitalised.

Time flew. Ten minutes before the end, the undercover coppers tell you all to stand up, that they are going to escort you over to the rest of the away support. Stewards gather at the top of the stand ready. The forty of you stand as one. The Hartlepool horde label you a bunch of wankers and shitters, but you don't care, this is the first stage of the retreat, the fall back to Dunkirk beach. The hard part, the bit like getting back over the Channel, is going to be getting to the train station.

You are marched over terracing full of cracked blocks, scattered rubble, patches of weed and exposed rusting metal jointing cable. You cannot believe how bad this ground is.

The steward ahead opens the gate, and you are reunited with the travelling Notts support, now resigned to losing one nil. You've not played well, but you don't care about that.

Your bowels are going because there are just six of you, and the train station is two miles away and it's pitch black, and you can see that the Pool hooligans in front of the away seats have all gone and you know they're going to be waiting outside.

Older Bully gestures to you and the other train trippers. He has a word with a steward who nods and walks you to the gate next to the old folk's stand where you found match tickets. He opens the gate, and you're out into the darkness. Hartlepool civilians, dads and sons, walk past you, the road illuminated by the floodlights, the streetlights and the un-curtained boardroom above. The locals are smiling because they've won and they don't notice you. You follow the two Bullys who walk against the flow of Hartlepool and up toward the main road.

You see Younger Bully stop. You look up the road.

Trotting down the white lines are fifty or sixty Hartlepool lads presumably on their way to the away exit gate. A young mob. Your bowels finally go, and all five of you are paralysed.

You turn round. Another twenty blokes are trotting up the other way. Beefy bastards in charity shop coats and steel-toe capped boots. Trapped.

You look at the Bullys, and they're not grinning this time. They're shitting it just the same as you. Bacchus is wide-eyed and stock-still. Gordon looks worried.

Asif clings to Older Bully's shadow like a limpet.

You look at him.

You know that if Hartlepool residents found it in themselves to hang a Monkey because they thought it was a French spy, they aren't about to give a sixteen-year-old Muslim the benefit of the doubt.

You realise that it's all over.

You're dead meat.

This is where it finally ends. Instinctively you wait for the punches to start raining in.

You can't run, you can't hide.

You're just going to have to fight to the death.

(It's your turn.)

Miraculously, a Black Maria rolls up to the kerb. Two coppers in front. Hi-visibility jackets. A lot older than you. World-weary eyes. Gordon seizes his chance.

He walks up to the window and taps on it. They wind it down.

Can you drop us off at the station, pal? Bit hot round here. They look at each other and they gesture to the back of the van. No jokes, no comments about Taxi services, no gruff insults. None of the usual copper stuff they do to pass the working day and to assert their self-appointed superiority. Just a nod to the back of the van. They must have known what had gone off today. The door is opened by another copper in the back. You follow the Bullys inside. Asif is grinning maniacally. It's the grin of colossal relief. He looks like he's taken a decent dose of cocaine. You're not sure you should celebrate because you've heard about Black Maria's Taxi Service. You don't care whether they nick you or not, whether you're actually on a one-way ticket to chokey, you don't care because you're off the streets. You don't know whether the approaching Monkeys had spotted you or not. Pointless. You'll never know. They aren't going to attack a Maria. Bacchus starts a conversation with the coppers in the back, a chat that goes nowhere. You all shut up. The sense of relief you feel is palpable. You could sleep. You could actually nod off and sleep. The van waits for fifteen minutes to check on the exiting away fans. When nothing much happens, the van drives off, arriving at the train station fifteen minutes later.

The coppers let you out of the van. There are no Hartlepool at the station, so you clean the buffet out, thirty cans of Stella and get on the next shuttle back to York. You're hungry, but you decide to get fed elsewhere. Best to get on the train. Soon you're off. You've somehow dodged a major bullet and you're elated, each of you downing a can straight away, then another, pitch black outside, talking about bollocks, delirious...

Chapter 7

Your dad died at the turn of the century. Over two hundred people turned up at the funeral at St Mary's in Arnold, and you cried. Only on the inside.

You loved your dad. Like many grafting dads, he never got to enjoy retirement. Worked himself to an early grave. Sat in his armchair one day, and passed away quietly. No pain. Your mum said he was watching Notts versus Brighton at Wembley on DVD, and he died with a smile on his face.

That was something, at least.

Just after Christmas, the second day back at work, you received a phone call from the Rose Meadow residential home.

It was from Amjit, the owner.

She told you that your mum had passed away.

She died peacefully, Amjit said. No pain.

She informed you that she died in the middle of the night. It was as if she made her own decision to go on her own terms. She was eighty eight, and you loved her.

You called Eunice and explained the situation. She seemed genuinely upset for you. You arranged compassionate leave of five days as you are entitled to as it was incumbent upon you to sort out her affairs and the funeral.

You engaged autopilot. You contacted relatives and family friends and accepted condolences, sincere or otherwise. You settled the account at Rose Meadow. You organised the death certificate and the Department of Work and Pensions. You hired a firm of undertakers that Rita's family have used for thirty years. You organised the funeral. You attended the funeral along with Rita and Perry, and thirty others. For once, you were a family and the three of you held hands at the graveside. The whole process took fourteen days, and when it was over, all of it, you told Rita you were having an early night, kissed Perry on the forehead (to his genuine discomfort), went upstairs to the spare bedroom, laid down on the bed and proceeded to sob yourself dehydrated all night and all the next day.

You realised that you were now your own man, completely and utterly - a significant milestone in a life.

During the grieving time, you didn't see Beanie and the lads, who you had been meeting regularly in the Pit. Rita was nice to you, the old Rita, the Rita who loved you and the two of you even had sex on two consecutive nights in your recovery - good sex, comfortable, warm, healing sex, something you needed badly.

For a week, you thought there was a chance that your mum's passing had brought life to a dead marriage, but sadly, it was just a hopeful phantasm. Rita became as distant as she ever had been and you suddenly realised that it was the first week in February and Valentine's Day was round the corner.

Work.

You've been struggling to keep your eye on the ball. You don't know what it is. You don't know why it is. Grief? Meeting the chaps? The hearing hanging over you? The slow decay of your marriage? Or the slowly encroaching sense of your own death, unconsciously interpreted through the slowly developing realisation of the *pointlessness* of your job.

Dying without ever having existed.

You survived your appraisal in January with little to spare just before your mum died. Margot gave you notice to improve and imposed a series of benchmarks and outcomes that you knew, with a changing marketplace and Tory cuts, were virtually impossible to achieve.

You said nothing. Merely nodded throughout the appraisal. You managed to turn a frank and open exchange of views into a dictatorial monologue. That suited Margot just fine.

Afterwards, you went straight to the pub to meet Beanie and some local Cotgrave shoplifters and side workers, one of whom hadn't had an on-the-books job since nineteen eighty-three.

The complaining customer still hadn't produced the necessary evidence. Margot still won't tell you who the customer is. Neither will Eunice whose relationship with you has deteriorated to the point where you no longer speak in the canteen. You know deep inside that there IS no necessary evidence, and the whole thing is a sham, an instrument of corporate control. To let you know that the company is watching. Twenty-four-seven. To make sure you will eventually make the mistake that forces you to resign.

No customer you know - and you've asked, subtly - knows anything about it. They like you and want to do business with you. The uncertainty nagged you and very nearly ruined Christmas. Now, you couldn't give a crispy duck.

Not a crispy.

There are more important things in life than work.

Homecoming Train

Later that night, Hartlepool, a fading memory...

You are at York train station. Younger Bully has finally decided to let loose.

Sober, you can have a conversation with Younger Bully. A pleasant conversation. You can discuss football results, the current state of the England team, the current state of *England*, fashion, music, the great Notts players of the past, but give him a drink and he becomes someone else, the ultimate Jekyll and Hyde. The complex compounds and enzymes in the booze travel straight to his lower brain, the unevolved slice that governs survival and predation, the kill or be killed zone. The stimulants and the disinhibitors in strong lager light up the untamed region mainlining straight into an evolutionary unconscious going back a million years. The snake brain is the part of the whole that governs the sex and fighting. Except, with Younger Bully, it usually skips the first bit and cuts straight to the ultra violence.

For some reason that's beyond you because you're a bit pissed, Younger Bully is threatening a bloke in a suit who is apparently going out on a stag party.

The bloke in the suit is not happy and says loudly he doesn't want any trouble. Bacchus has just nutted his pal who is lying on the floor moaning, holding his bleeding nose, which drips onto his white dress shirt. Gordon kicks him on the shin playfully. Asif is screaming in the face of another lad, no more than eighteen, in a pink shirt and trousers so beautifully ironed they could cut an apple in half. He doesn't want to know. He looks terrified. Older Bully is standing behind all this tomfoolery, smoking another cigarette and laughing.

The train to Sheffield arrives and you watch as Younger Bully tops off this grim Saturday evening tableau by punching the retreating suit in the back of the head.

He seems to believe the stag do consists of Leeds fans who like everyone else, he hates, but you cannot see any evidence for that, it's just a hunch, probably a bad one, and the five of you get on the 125 and head straight for the buffet car. You're hoping no railway coppers witnessed those appalling scenes on platform six. Plenty of shoppers did, some of whom have joined the same train to London as you.

You hope they don't grass. You suspect that like most of the country, they have habituated to the sight of young men battering the living shit out of each other at train stations on a Saturday night. The activity has become part of British culture, something an alternative tourist guide in foreign travel agencies could boast.

Come to Britain.

See ancient London.

Buckingham Palace and Hampton Court.

Visit Runnymede where King John signed the Magna Charta in 1215, thus germinating the process of democracy the world over.

The Houses of Parliament.

Nelson's Column.

The awe-inspiring Lake District.

York.

Royal Ascot.

Cheltenham Spa.

Snowdonia. The Peaks.

Witness the works of the immortal Bard in Historic Stratford-Upon-Avon.

Dance with Robin Hood and his Merry Men around the Major Oak.

Marvel at the sight of two hundred Stoke attempting to overturn a train full of Carlisle at Derby train station.

What would grassing achieve? Brutishness amongst English men so ingrained, it's hardly worth commenting on - this lumpen, unevolved violence.

Anyway, you hope they don't grass. It's a long way to come back to York for court.

So far, so good. The buffet car is packed, and you join the queue.In a carriage up ahead, you hear chanting. Millwall have been up at Newcastle, and Older Bully suspects it's them. Your blood turns to ice water. The ultimate legacy firm, you don't want to fight Millwall. You've just escaped the Sixth Circle of Hell and judging by the look on Bacchus' and Younger Bully's faces, you're about to jump straight into number seven.

Luckily (and surprisingly), Older Bully shakes his head.

Let's get some beer first, let the train get off, he says. It might not be Millwall, and in any case, they might be shirters. We have to be careful. They might wave a Match Weekly at us.

No one wants to fight with shirters. Fighting with shirters is like being caught having a wank.

The buffet car is full of students, civilians and women with carrier bags full of Christmas shopping. They're quiet, made quieter by your presence. Asif stands behind a bearded student and pours beer into his rucsac. Younger Bully tells him to pack it in, albeit with a grin on his face. It's your turn to buy the beer. You finally get served - fifteen cans of Stella, an order, which more or less, finishes off activities at the buffet. Gordon knows the girl behind the counter, and you get the beer for half price plus five shortbread fingers. The look passing between them suggests something more to their relationship than planning work rotas and stock orders.

She's okay. Bit fat for you - you like your women skinny, bony even, flat-chested, with no flamboyance. You don't like your woman to be noticed by other men. Or other women. The woman behind the counter is brassy and blonde, with huge breasts. Full of Yorkshire confidence. She's not for you, but Gordon winks at her. She grins back.

You ask for burgers - British Rail burgers being an unrecognised delicacy, particularly the British Rail cheeseburger - but she shakes her head.

All gone, nothing doing today.
Older Bully reminds you of Darlington.
Remember that buffet car on the way to Darlo.
You tell him that you do.
You were offered a job in a porn shop.
I know, you reply, grinning.
I think he fancied you.
You think so?

I'd have taken the fucking job there and then, he says, taking a huge gulp of lager. His eyes tell you that he's had too much to drink already, and this makes you nervous. He is dangerously unstable with drink inside him, and you're likely to get dragged in. You like your fighting in the ground. Older Bully is known for fighting on streets, in parks, in cinemas, in shops, in pubs and in nightclubs, anywhere where there are likeminded blokes about.

Didn't you fancy it? He asks.
Not really, no.
What's up, are you fucking bent? He asks with no hint of malice. I'd work in a porn shop for dole money.
No, I like my job as it is.
It was that lilac tracksuit top the bloke fancied. I could see it in his eyes.
The Ellesse one?
That's the one.
That's one of my best. I love that top.
I like that. Let's ey it when you've finished with it, mate.

You laugh and he does as well. You'd happily give it to him, but he's three sizes bigger than you are, and the pressure from his belly alone would pull the seams away from the whole.

Failing that fucker, he continues. I'll have that Cecil Gee jumper you wore at Gillingham.

You can't have that, Bully. That's Sunday best. You're both laughing. Bacchus joins in, and before long, everyone in the gang is baggsying items of your wardrobe.

Your burgundy and lime-green Pringle.

Your Caspian-blue Lacoste polo shirt.

The imported vermillion and rose Adidas tracksuit you wore at Northampton.

Your Forest Hills.

You willingly agree to pass out your whole wardrobe to your pals, but you draw the line at the Forest Hills with three gold stripes.

They let you off, knowing they've gone too far with the Forest Hills.

The buffet's a non-smoking area and the two smokers go off to find the smoking carriage.

Younger Bully wanders off to see who the lads are doing the singing.

Asif stands next to you.

I'm having so much fucking fun, man, he says.

So am I.

They're amazing, them two.

They certainly are.

Listen, he asks conspiratorially. Do you know what their real names are?

Not a clue. No idea whatsoever. C'mon, let's go and see who the firm is.

The two of you follow Younger Bully down the carriage.

You see him. He's sitting down with the mob, and by the looks of things, he's having a laugh. You gesture to Asif to come back, to leave him to it, and you take a position in the empty toilet space between the two carriages so you can keep an eye on him.

Before you know it, Younger Bully is joining in with the Millwall chants.

No one Likes Us! No one LIKES Us!
No one Likes Us! We don't care.
We are Millwall. Super Millwall.
Super Millwall. From the Den.

There are eight tables in the carriage and the shoppers and students around them look annoyed with the yobbish noise. You cannot see a ticket inspector.

Come to think of it, you haven't seen a ticket inspector all day. You could have travelled for nothing.

Surreally, Millwall start a conga up the carriage. Younger Bully has joined in with them and so far, it doesn't look like subterfuge, a bluff before the mayhem. He genuinely looks to be enjoying himself. The Millwall are the types of fan who go either way. Friends or fighting, they aren't bothered which. Old boys in their thirties and forties. Beer guts. Some evidence of sportswear, but nothing ostentatious. The conga comes past you, and before you know it, Asif and yourself have joined in, and the conga snakes down through the buffet car into the smoking carriages.

Let's All Do The Conga! Let's All Do The Conga!
OOH
Lalala LA. Lalala LA!
OOH

One-by-one, every football lad on the train joins in. The conga covers two carriages each time. All five of you are part of the conga, somewhere. The shoppers and students can't help but grin, even though they shouldn't. The conga turns and goes up and back down until the announcer signals the arrival in Leeds, and everyone returns to their seats.

You're not worried. Leeds are away at Portsmouth, and you're well mobbed up. Drunkenly, you sit chatting with Millwall about football violence and other enlightened topics until you reach Nottingham and then you get up, shake everyone's hand, find the smokers very drunk indeed, and before you know it, the five of you stand on Platform Three at Nottingham Station.

The station is empty apart from you.

Gordon lives in Derby, and he shakes everyone's hand and goes home. Asif lives in Beeston, and he shakes everyone's hand, departs, leaving you to contend with the

Bullys on the way into Nottingham to link up with the rest of the gang. These two have been known, like bored cannibals, to start fighting with each other over nothing, with no warning.

It is excused because they are brothers, but it makes for a nervous ten minutes as you make your way up through Broad Marsh, past the King John (the scene of many terrible fights), underneath the badly lit subway next to the bus station (the scene of many frightening brawls), up past the Sawyers, along the pedestrianised walkway to the Square (the amphitheatre of Saturday night mayhem for over a decade), and up onto Bridlesmith Gate. You see the metal walled utopia that is The Fountain - the Tortuga Inn of Nottingham City.

The boys are there, but the mood isn't good.

You get three pints of Becks in. You don't know the barmaid who serves you. She's new. She's mixed race, and you're immediately attracted to her. She's your type - angular and slim, with few bodily protrusions. You're not one for big tits, unlike everyone else in the firm. Beautiful brown eyes and coffee-coloured skin. Not too dark, milky coffee. You wink at her and call her darling. You're a bit pissed so you can't accurately assess her response. You think it's positive, but you can't be sure. You'll buy the next round and hope she serves you. Haxford, as usual, is there. Kent, Haxford's best friend is in. He didn't go to the game and is dressed for a nightclub. There's Preece, Clarkson, Breaker, Tom and a bruised and battered Little Dave whose face has inflated to twice the size. Ten or eleven others, including Wyckham, an old school hooligan from old times, and Dave Luke, an ex-miner who hangs round with the gang. They must have *flown* down the A1 to get here before you three, you think.

The pub is packed, but strangely subdued. The Fountain is Nottingham's top football pub and both local teams end up there on a Saturday night. It's traditional.

The pub is one big open plan room, with a lounge area furthest away from the door, fag-burned sofa-style seats snaking all along the back wall - for when you take the missus out - and the rest of it is standing room only. The impression is overwhelmingly beige. They play great music. Madchester sound. Old disco. Old Motown. They play at loud. It's a pea soup fog. Sherlock Holmes and Watson would be in their element. Forest generally drink on the other side of the bar. Notts stick to the top half, though you tend to be polite to each other in the toilets and at the bar, Nottingham being a small city. It's just not worth it, the constant aggro, not just on a Saturday.

Despite living in the same city as the oldest football club in the world, Forest outnumber Notts by four-to-one. Maybe five. This is all down to Brian Clough. All of it. It was roughly equal numbers until he took over at the City Ground. When the Reds started to do well, thousand of Notts jumped ship. All those old boys who went to Meadow Lane one week and the City Ground the next, stopped doing the former and started following Forest away. Before you knew it, you had become an ethnic minority in your own City. Open hostility is pointless. You are always going to lose with those odds. Nottingham is fun city, with three hundred plus pubs in a square mile-and-a-half, plus fifteen nightclubs and countless eateries. There are two football clubs, a world-class cricket ground, top quality horse racing, popular dog racing and international water sports at Holme Pierrepoint. London doesn't have this concentration of activity. Everyone goes out in Nottingham, and every night of the week is busy. They come from everywhere. Peterborough. Northampton. Banbury. Skegness. Buxton. Grantham. Harrogate. Whitby. Blackburn. Skipton. Huddersfield. You can bump into lads from all these places on the average Saturday night. Having the nature of a party city, Notts fans are always going to bump into Forest fans. You cannot avoid them. Every night of the week.

Naturally, because life is much too short, Notts fans behave like colonised ethnic minorities throughout history and conform.

You aren't happy about it, but what can you do?

You hear what happened outside? Tom asks.

No. We've just got back, you reply.

He shakes his head. He's drunk as everyone is, but not in a celebratory way.

Do you know Beechy?

Not very well, no. The Bullys are talking to Haxford and some of the others, presumably about the same subject. After a match like this one, it's difficult to talk about anything else.

How did you get back? He changes the subject, drunkenly.

You tell him a potted version, but you're curious. What happened to Beech?

You ask, getting his name wrong.

He lights a Benson, and he tells the story. The Printer comes to stand next to him, snarling as usual.

You've never seen anyone snarl as much as The Printer. Bacchus joins you.

After the match, we all tried to mingle in with the Hartlepool, Tom said. They opened the gates straight away, and most of us managed to get out into the road before their lads arrived. The car park is behind the away seats, and we'd been moved to the other side as you know. So we walk round past their singing stand. Their car park is vast. Our car is up the top, and we have to walk the full length. I'm walking on my own; everyone's split up. I'm shitting it. They are everywhere, walking up and asking people the time, people they don't recognise. I saw one lad look at his watch and then he's down, a right evil rabbit punch. I don't know who he is. The lad who went down, that is. I've never seen him before. They're savages, and they're out of their heads with anger. What do they hate Notts for? Does anyone know? I hate them bastards. Anyway, I know Beechy quite well.

Quiet bloke, lives up north, keeps himsen to himsen. Loves Notts. He's up ahead, somewhere. I walked into the middle of the car park, and I can see a scuffle. It's Beechy. I could tell that by the way he walks. The next thing you know, they're on him, whooping and shouting. There must have been thirty or forty of them, booting the shit out of him next to his car. Like ants. The only light came from headlights of cars waiting to get out. From where I was standing, there could have been up to a hundred of the Monkey hangers. All ages: Men, old boys, kids, teenagers. All them lads who were in the pub earlier giving it the big un. There's so many of them, they can't all fit around his body. They're *queuing* up to kick him. There's *that* many of the fuckers, they can't all stamp on him at the same time, Oh man, it was horrible. Anyone who went to help him was fucking dead, and I just walked past. Sorry to say that, but I did. He was beyond it. I heard some Hartlepool blokes try to break it up, and a big fat fucker in a donkey jacket put one of them on his arse. Horrible punch. I could hear the impact from a mile away. All I could see of Beechy was a pile of rags in a ball. He wasn't moving. His car door was open, and some of the Monkeys were raiding the glove compartment. They're even setting his car coat on fire while they're waiting to kick the fuck out on him. They're everywhere in this car park. It's freezing. They're slapping blokes behind me. They're slapping blokes next to me. They're slapping blokes up ahead. I saw one fella, a young lad I've never seen before, in a right state, sitting on his arse by the side of his car. He's bleeding from the eye. There's a man and a woman round him seeing if he was okay. I couldn't tell whether they were ours or not. How the heck we managed to get back to our car I don't know. Sheer luck. Sheer, sheer blind luck. I got ran at Lincoln when I was a kid. A friendly. Hundreds of the twats came at us after the match. I hid under a builder's van, and when it looked safe to come out, I popped my head out from underneath and there they were, ten of them. At least when they got me, I got a kicking and a few bitch slaps and they left me alone. They pissed emsen laughing, but these Monkey hangers were something special. They wanted to *kill* people. I've never seen anything like it. I tell you what, I've just spoke to that lot over there... he points to the Forest lads on the other side of the bar, out with their birds by the look of things...and them North-Eastern bastards are in for it whenever they come down here. Anyone from that part of the world. Boro. Newcastle. Sunderland. Hartlepool...

Clarkson said they were Boro.

More than likely, Tom continues. Plenty of Hartlepool. Seems like the whole town was there. Lots of them in the car park never went to the game. They spent the afternoon in that shithole of a pub.

Puts me off.

Puts you off what?

Going away.

Tom looks at you as if you're mad. Are you kidding? I'll never stop going. Mind you, I'll think twice about Hartlepool. I'd rather go to West Ham in a Millwall shirt than go there.

Breaker comes back into the pub. He's been to the callbox to contact his missus. She's been worried all afternoon. He tells us that there are eight Notts hospitalised. It's been on the news. She was relieved that he had phoned because she had been worried he was one of them.

In the Arriba Club later; after midnight, the place stinking of piss and pizza as usual. Drunk, listening to Rick Astley, trying to avoid a curvy bird who has you in her sights; a lacquered, skyscraper-haired blonde in a frilly, yellow blouse, colossal boobs, a big belly and jowls that store the winter hazelnuts for an extended family of fat squirrels. You're not in the mood, and unlike most of your friends out tonight, you're never in the mood to get stuck into fat birds. You hear from an older Notts lad you don't know very well in the upstairs bar, Swifty, a mate of Haxford's that the student Tom mentioned, the one sitting limp next to his car, had lost the sight in his right eye.

You don't know whether it is true or not.
You hope he's lying for dramatic effect.
You feel like death at the news.
It puts you off drinking and the night is over.
This isn't fun anymore.
This isn't harmless play fighting.
This isn't symbol.
This isn't rebellion.
This isn't a simulacrum of tribal conflict.
This isn't a connection to the medieval past.
This isn't the working class on the march.
This isn't pure, unadulterated entertainment.
This isn't a *laugh*.
This has become tragedy.

You also hear that after they kicked him unconscious, Beechy is in Middlesborough General.

They aren't going to release him any time soon.
You hope he's alright.
You also wonder, with bitterest irony, whether any of the Hartlepool scum rang him in the hospital to beg him not to grass.

Chapter 8

February 14th - Valentine's Day.

You're sitting in Clive's Restaurant in West Bridgford. Rita is opposite you. It's been a while since you've seen her in a good mood. She's not in a good mood tonight either. She looks beautiful, she always does, but she could have tried harder. You've seen her dress and shoes before, and her hair is tied back as if she'd just left the shower and is running late. You remember the times when Rita would buy something new for Valentine's Day. A new dress. A trouser suit. Makeup. She'd have her hair done.

Shoes, always shoes.

On one occasion, she even went on a pamper day at Byron's Manor up in Papplewick. Jacuzzi. Nails. Pedicure. Vajazzle wax. The pair of you went to Harts, ate the entire contents of the menu, went home and shagged until the streetlights turned off outside your bedroom.

Wasn't that long ago.

When you told her about the restaurant booking, and when you gave her the bouquet of roses and the chocolates, the lack of sparkle in her eyes told you that something had gone. Even her thank you kiss was as arid as a desert stone.

Still. You love her.

Even if she had turned up for the meal in a bin liner and a pair of Doc Marten boots, you'd still love her, and she'd still be the most beautiful woman in the room.

You're eating pan-fried breast of duck with cherry sauce and haricot beans. Rita has a rib-eye steak with hand-cut chips in a lattice, like Lego bricks.

There's a young man on a Hammond organ behind you. Incongruously, he's playing a Guns and Roses rock track in the style of a ballad. He's been doing similar hybrids all night.

Korn meets Mantovani.
Tony Bennett meets The Clash.
Jamie Cullum sings Black Sabbath.

Rita's hardly said a word to you all evening. You didn't really help matters by being late home, and you really shouldn't have had that last pint in the Pit, but you're sober. You can hold your drink, and you made the meal in time

You remember reading somewhere, that birthdays, Christmas Day and Valentine's Day were (counter-intuitively, paradoxically), the three most popular days for ending a relationship.

You wonder whether she's going to end it tonight.

The thought of her leaving you tugs like a fishing hook somewhere inside and your tortured innards are a mountain range that stretch into an infinite void. You can't imagine life without her, but you know it's coming. You can feel it, and for some reason, you cannot do a thing about it.

Maybe it's tonight.

Perry is stopping at a friend's in Hucknall. He and all his pals are apparently, going to be mixing some new tunes.

He told his mum this, not you.

You have the night to yourselves.

Clive's is one of the best restaurants in the Midlands and she's sitting opposite you looking as if you'd taken her to McDonalds after six pints at the Magic Spoons.

I have something to tell you, she says.

Your blood freezes.

You feel the urge to pee, but suppress it.

(*This is it, this is it, this is it.*)

I've been promoted at work, she says. I'm going to be Assistant Manager.

The relief shoots through you like electricity and you reach for your wine. You exhale audibly. Take a huge gulp. The couple next to you look over, but that may be coincidence. They aren't saying much.

That's fantastic, Rita. You raise your glass. She raises hers. There is a tinkle of glass congratulation.

I don't know whether to take it or not, she says. What do you think?

What are your thoughts?

You pretend to listen to her for the next half an hour, relieved that you're still going to have a marriage by the time you get home. You're not interested in her job in the slightest as you're no longer interested in your own, but each word she says is one word away from a divorce, one word away from Rita being with someone else.

You pray she continues. You order another bottle of red wine at thirty quid a pop and fill up her glass. She becomes more animated, talking about the people she works with, the political landscape of a modern office, the pros, the cons, the perceptions and the costs, and you sit there attentive. You can't remember pretending to being so attentive. You remember the first time.

The Fountain

Saturday evening. You start in the Bench and Bar at the top of the Broad Marsh escalators. When you walk in, the PA is playing *Step On* by the Happy Mondays, and you know that you are in for a good night. You've managed to get the last Football Post from that old boy whose been delivering the paper since the fifties. One day, you ought to ask his name. Preece, Clarkson and Breaker are looking at the League tables and discussing the prospects for promotion this year. Neil Warnock is doing the business for Notts, and the team is third in the table, looking good. The Magpies are hot and getting attention. Usually, Forest are the media darlings in Fun City, but nowadays they have to share the limelight. Not since Sirrel has there been such a buzz. Notts have some decent players and Warnock has them playing like a dream. Draper in midfield. Short and Yates, an iron backline. Bartlett up forward, scoring for fun. McParland flying down the wing and lobbing them in. It's worthwhile taking your eyes off the firms in the away pen. You couldn't often say that about following Notts.

The four of you drink pints of Becks. You could go home to get changed, but you've been out the night before and can't be bothered. You prepared in advance. You look alright, certainly on a par with the present company - a ribbed chocolate-coloured Armani roll neck, faded Levi jeans and jet-black loafers. You had only been playing a team of Muppets today and sure enough, the Muppets didn't bring more than two hundred, all cloth caps, mongs, shirters and women in big coats. There *were* four or five casual wannabes giving it the big one in the Norfolk, but you let some of the Notts drinkers from Bilborough slap them as they walked down the Canal while you and the rest went to the Navigation for a last pint before kickoff. Battering them would have been below you and you could have potentially ripped your Armani for no good reason.

It's warm out for the time of year, and dry. You drain half your pint glass in one gulp, and you feel it, the bulge as the liquid settles.

You've put weight on.

You look a bit like the rest of them.

Not all the way, but you're getting there. You've had to buy new jeans twice in the past two seasons because you've expanded from a thirty to a thirty four. On occasion, you can still get into a worn thirty two, but nothing top designer. That lot design for anorexics. You looked in the mirror the other day, and you noticed the beginnings of a double chin. Your mum has made a comment or two lately, when you go round for your Sunday lunch. Your dad hasn't noticed you in six months, such are the hours in his new job at the heating plant. You don't eat like an Ethiopian let loose in a McDonalds. The odd curry, the odd pea mix when you can't be arsed to cook. It's the booze, just the booze. Becks. Red Stripe. Stella. Southern Comfort and lemonade in Zaks, or the Arriba. Some of the Notts lads play football on Sunday mornings, but they haven't invited you to play yet. They may never do. Socially, these blokes are tough nuts to crack and the Sunday morning football is an inner circle, a closed group. Haxford runs it. You don't know why you've not been invited, you've known them long enough, and you've proved yourself on the concrete battlefields too many times to mention. Okay, you're crap at football - but how would they know that? It's another one of those rules that govern the way that men relate.

One day, they'll ask you. Or they may not.

You take another gulp of the cold Becks. You estimate this is your seventh pint of the day. Haxford and Crazy Jack wouldn't even consider that a dinner time session in the week. They'd go back to work after seven pints and put a shift in. You rub your belly hanging over

117

your crocodile skin Lacoste belt. You think of going to the gym three times a week, but with Notts and your travelling job, you're bolloxed when you get back to your flat and can't be arsed. You don't look too bad yet. It's not as if you're going to need to be fitted with one of those new gastric bands.

Not like some of the lads.

Your quartet sinks the pints and head for the Dog and Bear. You walk up Bridlesmith Gate, which is empty. Earlier today, it would have been rammed, one of the world's busiest shopping streets. You walk past Wardrobe. A squat meathead in a long black coat stands in front of the shop. Bacchus and his gang of brigands must have been at it. Meathead's been there all day, a throwback to a time when most human beings grunted at each other in strange code and avoided sabre tooth tigers by climbing trees. You recognise him. He's Forest, like all the bouncers round town. When they're not shagging sixteen-year-old girls from Basford, you can usually find them at the City Ground.

It's packed inside the Dog and Bear. Forest mostly, some Notts. No women - they generally don't come out until eight. You stand about while Breaker gets the ale in. The Landlord's invested in a new Fly's Eye rack of televisions. At the minute, it's showing a video of *Poison* by seventies relic Alice Cooper. That's been playing a lot lately, along with *Simply the Best* by sixties suspended animate, Tina Turner.

You realise that the nightmare, which is eighties pop music, has some way to go before it fades away. In any case, the jolly rock beat livens you up, and you are shocked to realise that you are tapping a loafer.

Four pints of Stella appear. The pub is solid with lads and it's just six thirty. You stand in the doorway and look outside. It's quiet, but by seven, the place will be full and by eight, heaving; difficult to get served.

More Notts arrive in the pub, and you drink up, the echoes of Depeche Mode's *Personal Jesus* in the ether, and you head up Bottle Lane to the QEII, a dank fleapit frequented by prehistoric pissheads and Forest. The pub is decorated with bottle green and whipped cream ceramic tiles, which makes the place look like an oversize toilet. It reeks, but it is tradition to visit the QEII, a link with Nottingham's past.

Too many pubs have shut lately, particularly the Flying Horse, with its ever-present smell of steak and its Minos labyrinth of rooms, each framed with ornately-carved oak beams and hardwood furniture, which was antique fifty years ago. Gone now.

And the Exchange, a Shipstones pub, minute, almost quaint, until you went inside, the back wall lined with fragrant and alluring Ladies of the night, sitting quietly, sipping Babychams, halves of lager and black, squired by hard-faced St Ann's gangsters, ear-ringed pimps with Stanley-blade decorated cheekbones. Visiting there was heady stuff for a kid. The Council turned a blind eye while developers turned those historic pubs into a yuppie shopping arcade for the Park set. Galleries, couturiers, jewellery shops. You can see the way the world is going. It won't be long before the QEII - with its toilet-influenced décor and permanent reek of piss, fags and bitter-slops - goes the same way.

And the Arriba above it.

There are plenty of you, Notts coming in all the time. Haxford is in there, along with Kent and Wykeham and the Skull, who is a Forest fan, a big mate of the Bully's and temporarily, adopted by Notts. There is no chance of a table, everyone standing, pints in hand. You're talking about football, the upcoming fixture down at Pompey; the fighting news from around the country; who's hot, who's not, who's rioted, and who's shat it.

Always football. Always football violence.

You hear that five thousand Birmingham destroyed the resort at Blackpool ensuring that countless civilian holidaymakers from Coventry to Tipton won't be welcome on the Golden Sands this summer.

You hear that Millwall battered Leeds at Watford Gap services. You hear that a coach load of Wolves held a copper hostage after a three-cornered battle between them, Hull, and Leicester on the M6. Hostage negotiators and armed police were called.

Carlisle's Border City Firm set light to the away stand at Preston, causing an evacuation.

Thirty-seven arrests in the ensuing fighting. Burnley and Reading fought a pitched battle in a Westfield Centre...

After a while, it all became wallpaper and yet the wonder never stopped, it was infinitely entertaining talking about fighting, you never tired of it, never *became* tired of it, you were experts in it, cultural commentators every inch as skilled and knowledgeable as the people on Panorama and World In Action. You knew every firm in the country, and you followed every snippet - whether urban myth, radio newsflash, tiny newspaper cutting, or rare TV footage - the news disseminated, as if by magic.

You finish your beer and the fifteen of you walk out of the pub in a line, walking past fifteen Bulwell lads, the fifteen Carlton lads, or a fifteen strong stag party from Stamford, all waiting to take your places. You go up the road to the Lord Nelson, but you don't stay there long because it's a bit shit and Haxford, who generally leads these endless crawls, is talking about crossing it off the list.

It's always crowded and the DJ carries on playing New Romantic stuff like the Human League and Tubeway Army, and Soft Cell, even though it's a decade too late and you may as well be listening to George Formby and his banjo.

The beer's rank, too, kept in dirty pipes too long. You visit the Nelson out of habit, the round, *the round*.

The round has an adaptive function. Latecomers and those who've gone home from the match to get changed know exactly where the mob is at any point of the evening. Most go home to change, they can get in a *proper* club somewhere other than the Arriba, anywhere other than the Arriba, which is a hole, albeit a lovable hole for degenerates and delinquents, and a social club for Notts.

It's not even eight thirty, and you're in the Fountain. You walk in, a long line, one after the other, past the bored bouncers who know you, but don't acknowledge you because they're too cool for that. *Ship of Fools* by World Party is on the PA system. The bar isn't too busy, and in any case, the Fountain put plenty on, up to ten bar staff on a Saturday night.

The barmaid you've been chatting up for ages is working tonight. She sees you and edges to the Notts side of the bar. Rita, her name is, and she seems to like you. It's been nine months since you got any and you're getting ready to ask her out.

Something always stops you. Not just with Rita. You don't know what it is.

You hope it isn't the obvious, you *pray* it isn't the obvious that it isn't the *condition that cannot speak its name,* but you don't think about that, you suppress it *right* down, deep into the memory banks and put a big smile on your face, a type of manufactured grin you believe makes you look cool and attractive.

Tonight, Rita is wearing hoop earrings and a cream lamb's wool v-neck top, which balances a tiny gold crucifix on a golden chain. She's wearing a denim skirt down to the middle of her thighs and Scholl wooden sandals.

There isn't an ounce of fat on her, with the exception of the beginnings of a lady tyre. That's quite fetching, you think. But you wouldn't want the tyre to get any more obvious. That would put you right off. She's got flawless legs, with no divots and scars, no scabs, or veiny trails. Legs are your big thing, and she's got sexy feet, tonight varnished violet with a gold toe ring bringing out her natural colour.

It's your round, and you order four Becks.

She asks you what town's like.

You tell her it's busy. Plenty out.

She asks what you're up to tonight.

You tell her the usual round. As if she didn't know.

She asks whether you'll be back in for last orders.

You nod. Always in the Fountain for last orders.

See you later, she says.

You suppress excitement. It might mean something, it might not. You can't read women. If you consider something like that an invitation when it isn't, when you strike, she'll pull away, asking who you think you are. The whole rejection makes you look a bit of an idiot, especially in front of that lot. Yet if you *don't* strike, she might think you're not interested: Next thing you know, she has her tongue down the throat of one of the top Forest lads.

The place is buzzing, and a queue develops outside, civilians in suits and loads and loads, and loads of women looking splendid and up for it. There must be three hundred people in the pub by eight forty five, and it soon becomes difficult to get to the bar. Rita is flat to the boards. Haxford is telling you and Tom about a ticket deal he has for Primal Scream at Rock City. You're only half-interested in Scream. Haxford is the type of entrepreneur who would buy and sell anything. Any ticket you want for any event, Haxford can usually find you what you need.

You know that if Notts ever got to Wembley, and it was a sellout, Haxford would have tickets. Not that he would sell them to anyone. He was good like that. He'd always sell to Notts first. He's tall, six foot, taller than you. He doesn't bother dressing up for matches and he rips the piss out of you and Breaker for wasting money.

He had referred to you as Gaylord, and you weren't happy, but that's Haxford, he rips the piss out of everyone. One of the lads in the firm was going out with a much older woman. Her name was Ginny. The gap was fifteen years at least. Coming back from one of the annual Blackpool weekends, Haxford's coach passes a cemetery. Look. He taps the lad with the older girlfriend on his shoulder. That's where Ginny lives. The target of his affectionate humour was visibly shaken. There are some vile nicknames going around, and most of them emanate from Haxford or Tom, who are pitiless in the face of weakness. Hax is the type of alpha-male who can get away with this kind of stuff.

He even rips the piss out of Older Bully.

But not Younger Bully. He's quite mild around him.

It starts to get uncomfortable in the Fountain with pockets of civilians barging into you and sticking fags in your arm and standing where you usually stand, and Haxford decides it's time to go up to the Malthouse. You'd much rather go to the Bodega behind it, but that's the price of running with the pack. There are at least twenty of you and you walk down Bridlesmith Gate mob handed.

You're pleasantly pissed and talking to Clarkson about something and nothing, and he's talking back to you about something or nothing, and you hear snippets of modern sounds from each pub you pass.

Gangs of girls ten strong in red high heels, and long coats, and fresh makeup, and thirty quid hairdos, and twenty quid clasp bags all the colours of the rainbow, smoking, laughing. It all seems to happen in slow motion as they walk past under the streetlights, and some of the lads know some of the girls. and waves are exchanged and implicit in the waves is an unwritten message of I'll-See-You-Later-In-The-Fountain.

The Malthouse DJ plays a Madchester song you don't recognise - Carpets? Scream? - and Breaker passes you a bottle of Newcastle Brown for some reason.

You look round to see if it's for someone else, but there's no one, the drink is for you, and this is the point of the night where you start hiding pints, giving the lads the impression you can stand your round and hold your drink when in actual fact, you'll be hiding pints behind statues and on the plinth near the toilets, no more than a quarter drunk because it's only just past nine, and you've got five hours to go at least, and you're not Haxford or Tom who, by a conservative estimate, have already downed fifteen pints since lunch in the Bentinck and you know, like a pair of Terminators, they are never, ever, going to stop.

You leave the Malthouse behind and head to the Bodega, and after that, you decide to go back to the Fountain for the last hour. By the time you get back, the place is half-full. You're well experienced in the rhythms of Nottingham's night life, and you know that the ebb and flow of drinkers usually leaves the Fountain free between nine thirty and ten thirty, so you strike, all twenty of you, and this time, the bouncers um and ah about letting you in, because you're all hammered, staggering, loud and boisterous, but Haxford has a word, and in you go, your corner free except for five civilians in moustaches, jackets, shirts, ties and trousers who are probably off to Madisons to try and pull. The gang encircles them, and the intimidated quintet move further down the pub.

Rita comes straight over, and you order two pints and two halves, the latter puff's duo for you and Preece, victims of far too much ale. She's definitely smiling, and you know you're in with a chance. She tells you not to go away, and that afterwards, she'll come out and have a chat, and you nod, buy her a drink, the money for which she puts in the communal tips tray.

You check your wallet.

You've well overdone it today, and you hope Rita doesn't want a late night curry because you'll have to borrow money, and you hate that.

You aren't paid until Friday, and you spent most of last month's salary on a black leather blouson from Ralph Lauren

You're in a situation.

You have enough money for a taxi and a couple more rounds in the Arriba Club. There's no way you're taking Rita to the Arriba.

Not on the first date. She's far too classy for the Arriba. The lads come over, get their beer, and admonish you for your tardiness. You tell them to fuck off, even though you hardly ever swear. They give it you right back.

Just at that moment, the Bullys come in the pub. They are in a right state, barely able to stand. You saw them this lunchtime in the Bentinck. There is a bouncer behind them, and he grabs Younger Bully and throws him out the pub, a flash of yellow. Older Bully follows. You leave your pint and stand at the door along with the rest of them. Younger Bully is lying flat on his back outside the pub and his elder brother is attempting to negotiate with the bouncers.

Lerrus in.

Cumon.

Ar mates ar in.

Cmon, lerrus in.

The bouncer pulls away, facing the full force of his booze and tobacco-smoke tinctured breath. They know the Bullys, but there is no way they are coming in tonight. Older Bully walks over to his brother and tries to pick him up. He is pulled down onto the floor, and the two of them roll about, half-wrestling, half-giggling. They try to stand, but they can't.

Look at that pair of dicks. Breaker says. They're like tramps! I'm ashamed of them. They're letting the side down.

Everyone laughs and agrees. Two policemen wander over to see what's going on, and this snaps the Bullys out of their stupor. They stand up, say sorry in a strange, drunken alien language, and say they will be on their way. It's not enough. A van drives up the pedestrianised walkway. Three coppers in hi-vis jackets get out and grab hold of the drunks, who are clearly too hammered to fight back. Younger Bully falls over in a stupor. He's a big lad, fond of a kebab and several pints of beer of an evening, and the coppers are going to have it all on to lift him up. Older Bully is trying his best to persuade the police to let them both go, but his entreaties aren't working.

None of you go out to help them because that would mean being unable to get back into The Fountain, and it's the best part of the night coming up. It isn't even discussed. All the women in the pub have enjoyed plenty of lager and black, and it usually goes straight to their panties. No one wants to miss that.

The Bullys are thrown in the back of the van and the bouncers shut the door to the disappointment of the queue outside waiting to get in.

They'll go somewhere like the Bench and Bar, where we started off. Maybe even the Nelson, to listen to Duran Duran or something irrelevant and ancient like that.

Rita comes over with half a lager and lime, and she stands next to you. Before you can even say hello, Tom, Clarkson and Swifty are all over her like fleas on a greyhound. They swamp her, and she's not averse to all the attention, even if it is drunken attention. Clarkson can scarcely breathe, never mind have a conversation.

The air is thick with cigarette smoke, and you are tired and irritable. You've had far too much to drink, and even if Rita wants to take the night further, you're going to be struggling.

The boys entertain her with pissed flirting communicated in an alien language. They spot three women they know by the cigarette machine. Amplebreasted blondes in black two-piece suits who look as if they've been drinking since last Christmas.

They seem to be struggling to remember the sequence involved in lighting cigarettes. One of them, with thighs like a footballer, puts the wrong end of her cigarette in her mouth.

They all laugh.

Like vultures, your friends spot the dead meat lying on the parched Serengeti and soon they're dive-bombing out of the azure skies.

You're alone with Rita. She's been to the toilets and dabbed perfume on. You don't recognise the brand. She asks whether you have a light. You say you don't smoke, and for a moment, everything looks less like the perfect jigsaw you want it to be.

Nevertheless, you've been out with smokers before, and you are sure Rita will have encountered the odd nonsmoker in her life. You let the jagged moment pass. She asks a nerdy-looking bloke in a blue-striped shirt for a light, lights her cigarette and taps you lightly on the forearm.

What are you doing after this?

I don't know, you say. I'm a bit pissed.

You?

I can see that. Your mates are completely hammered.

Football. It's all football.

Fancy a club?

Not really, no. I just want to go home to bed.

Oh, I do. I could do with a dance. All your mates are going to the Arriba. They've just told me. One of them asked me to go with him.

Who?

I'm not saying.

She winks at you. You're not bothered. Fun City is a free for all, and like the aftermath of a kicking or being arrested, it's every man for himself. You shrug your shoulders and watch Cher strut around an aircraft carrier surrounded by hunky sailors on the TV above you.

Are you going? She asks, probably aware you aren't going to say anything.

I usually do.

Are you going to take me?

If you want to go. The place is a dump.

I know the Arriba. I've been there a couple of times. Full of oldies, she says. She has that welcoming, playful face a woman sometimes gives a man when the two of them have crossed a Rubicon.

They don't play very good music, you say.

I don't know so much. I enjoyed it when I went. Me and me mates danced all night.

Round your handbag?

Rita moves closer to you. I didn't take a handbag, but yeh. We might have danced round someone's handbag.

You look at her and realise that she's a very good-looking woman, everything in proportion, beautiful big brown eyes and a lovely voice. Not much Nottingham in it. She might even be from out of town, you surmise.

Okay, you say, finally. You can come. That's if you know what you're letting yourself in for with this lot.

I'll be alright, as long as you look after me. She puts her hand on your forearm, and the sexual tension between you is palpable, but it might just be the drink talking. You stay impassive.

I'll try my best, you hear yourself saying.

I have to go and clear the empties and the ashtrays. Don't go without me. I'll meet you in twenty minutes.

Your friends disappear, tell you that they will see you later in the Arriba. A couple of them wink. You put down your half-supped pint of Becks and resolve to drink tonic water. Your vision isn't brilliant, and you feel bloated and sick. Your bed is a more sensible option than the Arriba Club, although that could be said of any Saturday night. You watch Rita scurry around. Plenty of attention comes her way, but she just smiles politely and carries on cleaning. A man can't be the jealous type if he chooses to go out with a barmaid: He'll end up in the nick, eventually.

Suddenly, your weakness hits you like a thunderbolt, and you start to panic.

What if she wants to go home with you?

What if she wants…

what if…

…you're not like the rest. They see a woman and their initial impulse is australopithecine. Hammer the wench over the head with a wooden club, throw her over an animal skin clad shoulder and carry her back to the cave, stupefied and passive. When it comes down to it, you appreciate women on an aesthetic level, like elaborate wallpaper or a particularly fine-looking painting. You can stare at a woman for hours, but history tells you that anything further and you become uncomfortable. It all gets a bit *tacky*. You're not comfortable with it. Your heart palpitates. You begin to panic. You feel as if you've eaten something dodgy from the takeaway. You adore the way they look, the way they dress, the way they talk. An alabaster sculpture on a marble plinth, illuminated by a crown of spotlights, something that you are able to examine from a discreet distance in three dimensions.

Tonight, you just want to look at Rita.

Watch her move.

See her dance. Feast your eyes on her coffee-coloured, perfectly muscular calves. You decide to keep her at arm's length. Engage her in a good conversation. Luckily, you can listen to a woman for hours and hours.

You love women's voices, feet, legs, the things they wear.

Sometimes you wish you were a woman. The shopping options, the makeup, *the shoes,* the lingerie, the underwear. Those little affectations with which they decorate a house, those things men never think of. Blokes just aren't catered for in the same way. You even have to travel to *London* to get some of *your* best sportswear!

You'd never discuss this particular point with the lads, though: They'd think you were a puff, and you wouldn't be invited to Pompey.

Rita comes over, a blackcurrant-coloured coat, a woollen cherry scarf and a subtle leather clasp bag that clearly cost a few quid. She slides her arm into yours, and the two of you leave for the Arriba Club.

Town is at its most vibrant in the hour between last orders and the long, slow walk to the nightclub. Illuminated by streetlights and the light escaping from pub windows, the place has finally completed its transformation from bustling shopping capital to a party paradise full of people loving the weekend.

There's no fighting tonight. The vans and policemen in hi-visibility jackets stand idly near the Council House chatting amiably to uniform groupies and cheerful pissheads. Everywhere, there is a smell of melted cheese, fried chicken, piping hot chips, hamburgers and hot chilli kebabs. Invisible cumin clouds rise above the curry houses. Takeaways doing great business from the all-day drinkers too hammered to get in Camelots. On a good night, which this is, revellers whoop it up in the streets. Partygoers joke, old lovers cuddle for warmth, and soon-to-be-lovers dance their enigmatic dance of anticipation. It's comfortably noisy. Music is everywhere, coming from every club doorway. Club queues snake down pedestrianised walkways like animated dominos. In the black sky above, the moon hovers, watching over proceedings like Old Father Time. You and Rita walk up Bottle Lane and join the queue for the Arriba.

They're playing *Ride On Time*.
You smile, and Rita asks you why.
Get your handbag ready, you reply.

Chapter 9

Rita excuses herself after her dessert of strawberry and champagne cheesecake.

You wonder when it was that you lost her.

You think about it for a while, but in the end, you have no answer.

You arrive home at ten.

Rita is tipsy but not drunk, but still, you don't hold hands in the cab. You make two filter coffees and listen to her talk. The television goes on. She gets the remote, tells you she's going to watch Coronation Street on rerun because she needs to unwind, all the talk about work has tired her out. You try to sit next to her on the sofa, but she tells you she needs to stretch out and you go over to the armchair.

Within ten minutes, she's asleep. You know her well. She'll be asleep all night. You go upstairs to the spare room and bring down the big twelve-tog purple double quilt guests use when they stay over. You place it on top of her, and you kiss her on the cheek.

You're numb, confused and on the verge of tears.

You don't know where you are.

You don't know who you are anymore. The tapestry unravels and there's nothing you can do to stop it transforming into a neat tower of fibre on the ground. You find your phone and sit on the stairs. There's a text message.

You call Beanie.

Heyup. Got your text. Where are you?

You can tell immediately that he's drunk.

Tahn. In the Bell. Out wi me missus. Remember Kaz? I don't suppose ya do. We've ed a rite gunite, worrabaht yo.

Great night. Bridgford. Just got in.

You in town tomorrah? He asks. Usual place.

Pit?

Baht twelve. Only talking abaht you today to Paul.

Paul who?

You know, Paul. Bus driver. Mad bastard, settled dahn nah, like rest on us saddoes.

I do.

He asked to be remembered.

Cheers. Same back.

We had a good chinwag. Do you remember Luton?

How could I forget Luton.

How could anyone forget Luton, buddy. Missus is staring daggers at meh. Reckon it's my shout. See you tomorrah, youth.

And you.

You put the phone back in your work raincoat and walk back into the front room. Rita is sleeping. You resist the urge - born in your confusion, no doubt - to lift up the quilt and touch her between her legs while she sleeps.

Instead, you find your laptop, insert your headphones, and select your nineties compilation.

You lie back and think of Luton.

Last Game Of The Season

May the Second. Nineteen Ninety Two.

The last match of the first division season, Luton Town. More importantly, the last match ever to be played in the old Meadow Lane, the rickety wooden stands soon to be a curious memory.

Nine thirty on Saturday morning. You look out the window. It's been raining off and on all night, and the sun is desperately trying to shine through the mashed potato clouds above.

You hope it succeeds: You don't want to wear a coat today, and you don't want puddles to ruin your new trainers.

You've just showered. Rita is still asleep, and you try your best not to wake her. You don't really want her nattering to you. Ordinarily, you enjoy it.

Not this morning.

You need to be focused and in the groove. You stick on your Sennheiser cans and listen to *Good Life* by Inner City. There is a busy day coming up. An important day in the history of Notts. You walk to your wardrobe. You take out a polo shirt - Lacoste, tangerine. Then you take out a citrus-green Sergio Tacchini. You put on a plain white tee-shirt and decide on the tracksuit top. You've never worn this one before, and you feel the demolition of the old Meadow Lane is a fitting occasion to introduce it to polite society.

You choose a ball of priest-black socks and your faded Aquascutum jeans. No accessories today - too easy to lose in a scrap. You sit on the edge of the bed and reach for the blue shoebox on top of the portable TV.

You open the lid, feel the lid separate from the case with a distinctive and reassuring wooomph.

You slowly separate the exquisite fine white tissue paper from the trainer inside.

You stare in wonder.

In awe, you remove a shoe from the box.

Smell the kangaroo leather.

Pinch the tongue of the shoe between your index finger and your thumb. Run your fingertip along the snow-white flesh.

You let your fingertip linger.

For a brief moment, you experience ecstasy.

Diadora Borg Elites with gold epaulette.

A classic eighties Shadey trainer and apart from Forest Hills, possibly the best trainer ever made. You discovered the pair on a London shopping trip, in a Vintage sportswear shop just off the Portobello Road. Never worn. Still in the box. You paid twenty-seven pounds for the pair and you consider it the bargain of the century. When they first appeared in Nottingham in 1983, they were over forty quid. In the middle of Thatcher's vengeful recession, the worst recession since 1933, no one could afford forty quid. Only nine years ago.

Now you can afford it.

Veni. Vidi. Visa.

You came. You saw. Out came your credit card.

You put on the trainers. They feel like a carpet would feel underfoot in heaven. You walk over to the full-length mirror in your bedroom and admire yourself. They are virgin white, not a scuff or a mark on them, and the gold stripes on either side seem to sparkle in the morning gloom.

You look the business.

You turn the music up.

Big Fun by Inner City.

For the duration of the tune, you are in a different world.

Rita is still asleep. You've been seeing her for over two years and the pair of you have discussed marriage. She no longer works at the Fountain as in a fit of the red mist, you slapped a lad who was chatting her up. Actually, you battered him.

Absolutely battered him. Left him a bit of a mess. Being in your year at school ensured he got the full treatment. He wasn't one of those who kicked the shit out of you that day, but in your mind, he was associated with them and thus, you saw red outside Birdcage.

Blood everywhere. The lads had to pull you off.

Rita finished with you.

The beating looked much worse than it actually was - nosebleeds can do that and your school was a tough academy - but you still didn't blame her for finishing the relationship.

You were upset about it. You were in love with Rita. Still are. In the aftermath, you drank a lot, put on more weight, went out every night to the local, to various locals, to the midweek matches. You even considered sleeping with another woman in the Wheatsheaf in Broxtowe. In the end, your heart wasn't in it because she had fat earlobes. You couldn't stop looking at her earlobes, even when she was trying to kiss you. You weren't aware up until that point that earlobes could store fat deposits. Those earlobes put you right off.

You further soothed your heartbreak by fighting with fifty hard-core Yids at White Hart Lane (after they scored a disputed winner following eight minutes of injury time).

After a month, Rita called you.

You went for a drink. You made promises, which you've kept, and she finished working behind bars. She works in an office. Credit control. She enjoys it, and she gets weekends off. You helped get her the job through a contact - with more than a little self-interest in mind. She doesn't like you fighting at matches, but giving that up wasn't part of the deal. She knew what you were before the two of you got together.

It's a simple and very basic rule in a relationship. You get what's there, not what you'd *like* to be there.

If a man chooses to go out with pretty woman, who just happens to be a confirmed slag incapable of keeping her legs together when men are anywhere about, that man cannot complain if she's unfaithful to him. Any ensuing heartbreak and misery isn't *her* fault. It's his.

It's the same with Rita.

She knew the score about the fighting in advance. She knew what was *there*.

You love fighting at matches. You have done ever since you saw the Cardiff Orc coming toward you on the Meadow Lane turf all those years ago. It's in your DNA. You cannot stop it.

There are certain things about you that appeal to Rita. You're intelligent. You're not short of disposable cash. You shower and shave. You're faithful. You don't beat her up. You try to ensure she finishes first. You don't forget her birthday. You don't forget anniversaries. You buy her nice presents. You visit her mum once a fortnight, on a Sunday. You, occasionally, go shopping with her. You are a better listener than you are a conversationalist: When she's off on one about her job, the people at work, you sit and listen patiently, let her get it out of her system.

As for compromise, if she asked you, if she *really* wanted you to, you would stop drinking with your mates on a Friday night, you would stop dabbling with drugs, cease your occasional requests for anal sex and - your biggest potential sacrifice - kick your habit of buying extremely expensive sportswear.

You could give up any of these pleasures whenever you felt like it, and you would do. Easily. You would stop all this, if she wanted you to, if she put a gun on your temple and threatened to pull the trigger. You would even stop watching the ac*tual football* itself, if you were forced, and definitely programmes like Match of the Day, but there is no way, no way in the world, you could ever give up fighting at football matches.

It's just impossible.

Don't ask me to stop, you asked, and she hasn't.

She's come close, the closer you and her become, but she's never said the words.

It's a good job, really. You'd have to disappoint her.

You find your wallet and cram it inside your front pocket. There's a hundred quid, and you have another two hundred in the bank if things get tight. This is a premium game with no half measures. You don't expect to be back until three or four in the morning. You sit down next to Rita and kiss her on her shoulder. She smells like an angel in the morning, and a part of you wants to get under the covers and mould your body into her intense warmth. You suppress the thought. She's out with her sister tonight in town and you might bump into each other later. She stirs as you kiss her, but before she can say anything, you're off and running. It's a big day and time waits for no man.

After today's game, the builders will level the old ground and rebuild it, an all-seater - the first phase.

Advance builders had already been in. Half the Spion Kop end is already history.

It would be the end of an era. No way would Notts ever attract 47,000 as they did at home to York in 1947. Crammed into the kop like sardines, kids passed overhead down to the front.

Lawton *hovering,* like an eagle.

Football needed to change with the times and Notts - a tiny club without cash, punching above their weight in the First, relying on the largesse of ex-Forest Director and local plumber's merchant Derek Pavis - had held off the expensive inevitability as long as possible. Sensible supporters you know say redevelopment should have been enforced years ago. Not just for Notts. Feet have dragged in FA Towers. Bradford's horrifying fire, the riot at St Andrews, the horrors of Heysel and most tragic of all, the crush at Hillsborough should have rapidly inspired legal change, the century of rotting, woodworm-infested holes fans call stadia made extinct. Locks and chains on hundred-year-old iron gates and a boom for the demolition gangs. You weren't sure. The alternative - of soulless, out of town, all-seater stadia, close-circuit TV on every stanchion, new police powers - the new football SPG; bored servers in paper hats wandering the seats, carrying cool boxes full of pretzels and Pepsi: *Simply The Best* accompanying the teams on the pitch, buxom cheerleaders in the centre circle at half time and full body searches at the turnstiles - didn't get the pulses racing either.

Nevertheless, some of *that was* going to happen to the Lane, and there was nothing you could do about it.

You get on the bus, noticing several kids assess your gear. You don't mind. That's what the gear is *for*. It isn't just the dead ground that makes the upcoming match a potential classic. Luton need to win to stay up, and the grapevine tells you four thousand fans are making the short journey up the M1.

Including the MIGS.

The Men In Gear.

Luton's lads, a hundred to two hundred strong.

Every Notts lad worth his salt will be out today as The Hatters enjoy their Nottingham day out. You've all arranged to meet up in the Fountain at eleven. You expect at least fifty of you to be present and correct. Not a lot, but you're only a small club.

You know the score. It's enough. Fifty handpicked men can do maximum damage in the right context. Notts has nothing to play for today except pride. A week ago, the First division dream had ended in a nightmare at Maine Road. Man City relegated Notts on the pitch and for the second time this season, ran your firm down the back of the Kippax, into Moss Side, and back into the city centre.

Of all the legacy clubs, City is the *bête noir* for Notts. Especially after 85 when they virtually wrecked the Notts part of the city.

That day, City needed to win to gain promotion to the First Division. Followed by ten thousand Mancs, most crammed behind the towering and foreboding fences in the Kop, but plenty all over the ground. Most of the seats were full of City, creating a hostile atmosphere, a stick of dynamite with a hovering flame waiting to light a short fuse.

Their crimes started at midday: The historic Norfolk and Gordon pubs wrecked before the game. Groups of Notts supporters beaten and chased. Two middle-aged blokes, an architect and a chartered accountant, lifelong Notts, chucked in the canal that runs along London Road. Widespread robbery. A petrol station set on fire. Many Notts fans turned round and went home, fearing for their safety. Most Notts fans at the ground hoped that City would win: Heaven help Notts County if City lost. It was a tinderbox.

Naturally - the God of Irony being a mischievous god, with a vicious sense of humour and an impish sense of fun - Notts went three nil up in the first thirty minutes. Cue riot.

By the third goal, City was all over the Roadside seats. Battering shirters, scarfers, men in raincoats given complimentary seat tickets by reps, workmen in overalls just finished a shift at Eastcroft. The Bovril makers behind the hatches, old stewards in NHS spectacles and cloth caps, homely women in big coats with flasks and strawberry Panda Pops for the kids.

A team of market research students from Nottingham University standing at the bottom of the stairs, oblivious, their plastic clipboards scattered to the four winds. Whole families - crying kids, scared little boys, terrified little girls. Anyone with a black and white scarf was fair game for City. They slapped anyone they could lay their hands on.

They say on the grapevine that Notts threw the game to prevent further mayhem and maybe, even death.

In the end, it was 3-3.

You hate City as everyone else at Notts does.

Even if Notts fans don't hate City, they should do.

The dislike extends beyond football. You don't like Manchester much because of that game. At work, you avoid talking to Mancunians of either stripe, City or United, as much as possible.

You do most of your business down south and in the east. Your boss has learned to send Gilbert to northern meetings.

The only upside of last week's relegation is that today, the pressure is right off, and Notts fans can have a party. By contrast, to stay up, Luton needs to beat Notts, and for Villa to beat Coventry at Villa Park. Maximum pressure. It is all set for a top day out, and you're buzzing like a bumblebee high on nectar.

It's not quite ten thirty, and you stop off at McDonalds for a breakfast. The Bullys are sitting quietly, reading their papers. Older Bully gestures you over. You order bacon and egg McMuffin and a small coffee.

The brothers are having a full set. A full breakfast each, plus a Double Bacon and Egg McMuffin, a Double Sausage and Egg McMuffin and three extra hash browns. Both have a large Sprite in front of them, as well as their orange juice and black coffee. You sit down next to Younger Bully because Older Bully smells as if he's spent the night in a skip outside John Players. Rumour is that he's a teacher, but no one believes it. If he weren't overweight, he could be mistaken for a tramp living at Emmanuel House. He's wearing a pink Ocean Pacific surf tee-shirt with a fag burn in. The original has a sunglasses pocket and in it is a packet of Embassy Number One cigarettes. His sunglasses - imitation Wayfarers - are on top of his head. He has a wedge haircut, like yours, and it's been recently cut, but not looked after, unlike yours. His eye sockets are completely black from lack of sleep and over-indulgence. A chunk of scrambled egg on his unshaven chin, next to a dab of tomato ketchup and he's spilled coffee on his tee-shirt. The sight puts you off your sandwich, and you wished you had sat next to him - at least you wouldn't have to watch him eat. By contrast, Younger Bully looks positively refreshed. He's wearing a royal blue short-sleeved shirt and an expensive wristwatch. He resembles someone off to a pleasant concert by the river. You resist the urge to ask their first names (you cannot help it), and the three of you talk generalities; most importantly, the planned fighting today. They are both anticipating a major battle around two o'clock down by the City Ground. They have previous with the MIGS on their patch. Not good previous.

Debts have to be repaid.

The three of you finish breakfast, mop up with tissues and walk out onto Bridlesmith Gate. Shoppers clog the pathways, and you negotiate a path with the tide down toward The Fountain. A homeless with a beard and a crazy-quilt sweater sits begging outside a sports shop. You think you recognise him, but you know you're being silly. No one you know will ever become homeless. You notice more and more tramps sitting by the sides of the walkway, begging. You've heard that tramps from all over the country have arrived in Nottingham recently because they've built a huge new homeless shelter down on London Road.

Seys Law.

You know this from your economic history module.

Seys Law. Demand rises to meet supply.

Build it and people will come.

Spend a hundred million on a new hospital and before you know it, ill health increases enough to create a yearlong waiting list.

Spend a million on a homeless hostel and you'll get double the homelessness you had before.

It's a curious concept, and you have no idea how to solve the problem, so you forget about it and follow the Bullys.

Outside Barclays Bank, you spot four Luton queuing at the cashpoint. Lads. Tracksuit tops and roll-neck jumpers. Trainers, but nowhere near as good as your Borg Elites. As if by magic, they turn round and one of them spots you. It's your tracksuit top. The Bullys gesture to each other imperceptibly. Shoppers walking past are completely oblivious to the psychic communication going on in their midst, code known only to hooligans hiding in plain sight.

They've been sussed and so have you.

Tension builds.

Older Bully walks past one of them in a bright-pink Fila polo shirt and shoulder barges him. There is a standoff. Adrenalin shoots through your system generated from a standing start. You don't expect this. Neither do they, by the looks of it. You face each other, a gunfight without guns. Three versus four. Harsh words are exchanged, but there is an unspoken understanding developing between the two sides - more psychic non-verbals - that it's far too early for a set piece. It's not even eleven. There's bound to be filth about. Plenty of it, as well. Last thing any of you want is to spend the afternoon searching for the face of Jesus on the shit and graffiti-stained cell walls down at Central.

You carry on, walking slowly to the Fountain, past Birdcage, the seven of you exchanging wanker signs and insults, watched by startled couples and unamused shoppers. Promises are made of a meeting later round the ground.

You've crossed a Rubicon and the three of you are now on the clock.

At heart, you're all football fans. You started out watching football at the Lane with your dad. You started playing football on the Rec, twenty a side, jumpers for goalposts. In your head, you were Tony Currie or Frank Worthington, spraying forty-yard balls to the wings as if shelling peas. You dreamed of being a footballer. Up until that time, you realised you were never going to make it at football - that you were, in fact, a bit shit - that dream remained potent and kept you from sleeping soundly. You love football, ultimately. The fighting is a lucky by-product, added-value entertainment. Sometimes, you get matches you're not interested in spoiling by having a scrap.

Matches where you like the opposition fans, like Portsmouth and West Brom.

Matches with decent football teams.

Matches where you want to kick back and savour the splendour. If Notts ever played spiritual brothers Juventus, for example, or Dutch maestros like Feyenoord, or Ajax.

Notts versus Luton is not going to be one of those matches.

Today is going to be total warfare.

It's not going to be a day out for crybabies.

You walk into the Fountain, and it's like a Who's Who of Notts County Hooligandom. Everyone has turned out for this, and there's a good atmosphere. People are dressed smartly. The Fountain has been done up, the metal wall outside replaced by a glass window more akin to an Italian coffee house. Another sign of the times. The place is cleaner with more video screens, and chairs you don't need to wipe with a wet tissue before you sit down. The beer's more expensive, but then it all is nowadays.

The front half of the pub is rammed. Haxford buys you and the Bullys a pint of Becks each. Preece comes over, and you tell him what's just happened. As usual, he's wearing an unbranded black V-neck pullover, civilian shoes and smartly pressed jeans.

I'm really up for the cunt today. I'm desperate to smack one of the Luton cunts, he says.

You'd have enjoyed it outside, you say.

Got slapped down there this season. Dropped. Ambushed us at the station. MIGS. Bastards.

How many do you think they'll bring.

At least three. Probably four.

We're in for a long day, Preece, you say.

On the video screen above the bar, Nirvana bangs out *Come As You Are* and the pounding guitars seem a fitting accompaniment to the prevailing mood.

You finish the pint Haxford brought for you in one. You start queuing at the bar. Your ability to drink amazes you.

To think when you first started, you couldn't drink three pints without your head spinning and talking bollocks. Now you can make double figures plus.

That's the true legacy of following Notts.

You look round at some of the assembled while you wait. A roll call. There's Breaker and Jinx, and Fletcher and Rodders, and Stuart and Beanie, and Clifton James and The Printer, and Tom and Haxford, and Crazy Jack and Nicky, and all the Pauls and Swifty, and Little Dave and Preece, and quite a few blokes Haxford's brought down with him who you know by face, but not by name. There's Madman and his mates in the corner, discussing something animatedly. There's ten Arnold you went down to Brentford with, now nodding acquaintances of yours. The Newark mob is supposed to be linking up down the station, but you recognise a couple of them already here. Whisky Jack. Jimbob. There's Swifty, Wykeham. Dave Luke, and Clarkson. The four of them look ready to go out to a club rather than a match. There's you, the Bullys, Godfrey, Asif, Bacchus and

Gordon. There's Ray Banner, the old sea dog, sitting quietly, talking to a younger lad. He was one of the first, in the sixties. He doesn't like attention. You don't go and pay your respects. You leave that to the people who know him.

Fifty handpicked men.

You drink, chat, and feel the rising anticipation for an hour and then it's time to go.

To avoid the attention of the coppers, you leave ten at a time in two-minute intervals. You decide to stick with the Bullys who are still drinking their pints. The pub empties slowly and soon, it's your turn to walk out into the bright sunshine. Preece joins you. The six of you walk down Bridlesmith Gate and through the top entrance of Broad Marsh, past the Bench and Bar. You're keeping your eye open, but know that most Luton will be on the other side of the Mall. You see flashes of orange everywhere, but it's usually just a shirter looking for somewhere to buy replica Subbuteo souvenirs. You go down the escalators and walk past the Wimpy. Broad Marsh is solid with eager shoppers and you're reminded of the fights that have seen these very same shoppers scatter like startled fish in a bowl, as a Sunderland or a Chester mob, start fighting for their lives outside the comic shop - the shocked faces, the resentment, the moral outrage, the recriminations, the letters to the editor. You go down another set of escalators, and you're into the bus station, the six of you. You can see Clarkson and some of the others up ahead, next stop, The Bentinck, which is bound to be full of Luton.

The King John near the taxi rank is sometimes an away fan magnet and you tense. You trot toward the entrance to the sixties bus station, a foreboding, dirty place, stinking of piss and bad memories, an arena of hopelessness and countless brawls. Bouncers and Cops seal off the pub, but there's plenty of Luton in the pub staring through the windows.

Wanker signs are exchanged. The doors are immediately shut to prevent Luton getting out, and you grin at the lads in the window, blow them kisses, their contorted faces of rage. You walk up to the Bentinck, but you stop at the traffic lights. There are vans and about ten standing coppers outside the pub in hi-vis jackets.

MIGS.

That's where they are.

You'll never get in the pub, and you'll end up in Central with that level of filth scrutiny. You take a left and walk down to Station Road via Canal Street. You've merged with another ten Notts. Any Luton wandering around unable to get in a pub will be up for it, and the games will begin.

It's half past midday in warm sunshine, a tantalizing breeze. You're walking down toward the Norfolk. A huge crowd outside enjoying a pint and the weather. They're mostly Notts. A few Luton shirters discussing David Pleat and team selections, as if either of those things matter in the last game of the season.

Or ever, to be honest.

Thirsty, you stop off and queue for a drink. All the Fountain lot are in there or outside. There is sporadic chanting from the Notts shirters. Luton pass by frequently on the other side of London road, but nothing spectacular. No MIGS. They're either in town or on Trent Bridge. Traffic is heavy heading toward the bridge and the exhaust fumes leave a sticky haze. It gets in your throat, and you drink your Becks that much faster.

You listen to Living In A Box on the jukebox.

The Blow Monkeys, *Digging Your Scene.*

Finally, someone puts on *Party Fears Two* by the Associates and you're beset by nostalgia for the old days.

Everyone is talking animatedly, except you. You're taking in the atmosphere and waiting for it to kick off.

147

You're tense, but not stressed. With the drink, you're experiencing taut anticipation.

Nottingham is a jungle at moments like this with enemies waiting to ambush you behind every tree. You love it. You can't get enough. You look over beyond the canal on the other side of London Road. Past the giant car showroom, the army surplus compound with its jeeps, tanks and rocket launchers. A post-industrial landscape of industrial units and storage warehouses stretching down Meadow Lane all the way to the heights of Colwick Woods. To your left, Eastcroft pumps out its diabolical gases. A suggestion of sulphur in the air - something to accompany the exhaust vapours. They say that mercury and potassium leaked from the plant into the canal last year and killed all the fish. The atmosphere gets in your Becks as you take another sip. Up above you, the sky seems immeasurable, cobalt blue, a single cumulus cloud searching vainly for company. For a moment, all is silence, the volume of the cacophonous commotion around you turned right down. On top of the lawn mower factory, a lone Kestrel watches the fishermen passing time away on the canal and waits for the right moment to strike. He doesn't know that all the fish are dead, or maybe that was just a rumour.

You smile. Sip your Becks. You feel peace.

Oneness.

You are at one with the world and...

...Preece taps you on the shoulder and tells you that Notts are all heading to The Aviary, the fun pub on Trent Bridge to kick some Luton cunt's head in.

You drink up, and before you know it, there you are walking down London Road as one of two groups of Notts, an impressive turn out. There is a mood of determination. Everyone is ready. There will be no running today. You and the mob might get seriously pasted by well grouped superior numbers, but you will go down fighting and take a few Luton with you.

It begins swiftly, spawned as if from nowhere. You walk down to the traffic lights leading to the Aviary. You see twenty of them walking right toward you, not stopping, full of drink and Dutch courage. Jeans and jackets - non-casuals, maybe a coach load of pissheads. You all stop. Across the road, outside the front entrance to the Aviary, you notice two coppers reach for their radios. Clarkson and Preece are at the front.

The Luton walk toward the approaching throng. Preece slaps a bloke with a moustache, and he stumbles. It goes off, a high pitched, frenetic kaleidoscope of fists and boots, and nuts and shouting, and finger pointing, a disorganised, uneven, patchy mess, nothing artistic about it, a scrum, but a release of the tension, nonetheless. The two coppers race over, breaking it up. With teams like Luton and Notts, two coppers can break up a mini-riot. You don't manage to get a punch in, and you're momentarily pissed off about that. You all scatter, some on the road, some sprinting toward the pub, others standing there giving out the signs. Luton do the same, a mirror image. Miraculously, in a feat of navigational brilliance, the Luton have managed to completely swap places with Notts so that they are the ones closer to the ground. They carry on walking. Preece is well pleased with himself though he's taken a solid punch, his cheek red and flushed.

As you are about to walk into the pub, Younger Bully taps you on the shoulder. He tells you to forget the Aviary and gestures to come down to the Sportsman outside the Forest ground. You nod and walk back on to the bridge.

This is the scenario the Bullys like best.

Inferior numbers and rapid mobility. The old Chindit tactics behind enemy lines in Burma. Older Bully tells you he's seen a posse of MIGS head toward the Sportsman. Filth wouldn't let the fifty get across the road, but ten handpicked men would get away with it.

He has a faraway look on his face as he speaks and for once, no cigarette.

The two coppers who had just stopped a major punch-up seem to have missed these new developments and the ten of you merge with the traffic. The river is twenty feet below you, boats, canal cruisers, canoes full of Nottingham University Blues and families of ducks in easy Spring transit, the floodlights of the City Ground up ahead on the skyline. You turn the corner past Cheers Bar, and you see them. Big lads - not kids, not shirters, *lads.* Casuals. Skins. MIGS. Drinking outside the Sportsman, the Forest Private Members Club. The Bullys gesture and you trot toward them and up ahead, you see the Luton put down their pints and come down the steps. There are no coppers and its going to go off, and they run toward you, no showing off the sportswear, straight in for the fighting, the lunchtime beer kicking in and the weeks of anticipation, the pub chats, the dreams and the fantasies, the last game of the season.

Kick off. There is a collision, a crash of bodies. You're straight in. You lamp a bloke in a denim jacket who is much taller than you are and he goes down, a weird look on his face as he hits the tarmac. Karma waves her magic wand and you are floored by a right hook from a bloke in electric blue cords and a mop top. You feel your tracksuit top rip, your elbow sends a pain signal to your brain, and you squeal. Two other blokes jump you in a flash of colour (Ellesse? Diadora?), you think as you go down under a flurry of slaps and boots. Younger Bully levels one of them with a glorious right-hander and Gordon headbutts another before he's clipped a good one with a ring, and he bends over screeching, clearly cut. You're off the ground, enraged, swinging wildly, connecting, missing, connecting, you can feel blood on your lip, your nose smarting, and just as it starts to get interesting, a squad car comes round the corner, sirens blazing. Everyone on their toes, back on to the bridge, Notts and Luton, no one wanting to get nicked, a paradoxical amalgam of cooperation and navigation developing. You sprint across the bridge, and there are coppers running down past Cheers, the stable door shutting after the horse has bolted.

You head for the Aviary along with Preece, and Gordon, and Bacchus, somehow - and miraculously - Notts have managed to merge on one side of the bridge with the MIGS remaining on the other - examples of psychic communication and non-verbal behaviour under pressure, the tribal homing instinct and navigation-system working overtime. You run inside the Aviary before the coppers can work out what's going on, and who is who. The pub is packed, a mixture of Notts and Luton, milling about inside and out. You don't bother getting a drink and sit on a wall overlooking the car park. Gordon comes over to you. You thank him for helping you out. The ring has cut his face, but not that badly. A mob of cops arrive in the pub and you grab a newspaper conveniently left amongst dinner plates and dirty glasses, and you sit down, pretend to read. You take off your sadly-ripped Tacchini tracksuit top; after today, a write-off, an inauspicious debut performance. You become just another civilian with a wedge enjoying a burger and a Saturday afternoon out. *Football? Wot, me, guv?* Gordon flicks peas around a dirty plate. There is a melee in the pub as the coppers march out two blokes, neither of whom you recognise, neither of whom had been anywhere near the Sportsman, earlier. The Rozzers need a result for all the running about and anyone will do. There is consternation and denial. Gordon says they'll probably just put them in a van for ten minutes, rough them up a bit and let them go, being filth. You agree with him.

Before long, you're all ready to go. It's two pm and time for the Navigation Inn. Rather than attract the attention of the bill, you break into groups of three and walk across the road to the new collection of Yuppie flats on the canal.

Turney's Quay. If you have to ask how much one of these ponceboxes is, you can't afford it.

You walk across the walk bridge, through the Brookside-style communal road, and down the alley to the Navigation, which is teeming with Notts. There is no chance of a pint as they are queuing five deep at the bar. There is chanting and singing outside. The Bullys have four pints between them, holding two each. There's Tom and Haxford with similar. You don't really want any more beer. You're too busy buzzing. Everyone is out of it and singing Notts songs. Word of the Sportsman scrap has got out. Someone will tap you on the shoulder. There are no Luton to be seen.

At two forty five, you decide to make a move. The Bullys drink up and the three of you walk down Meadow Lane past the condemned Cathedral.

You look inside - it's jammed. There are at least fifteen thousand, but you'll never see that figure in the Sunday papers. More like eight with Notts keeping the cream away from The Revenue. Luton has filled the old home side of the Kop and a sea of orange accompanies a ferocious wall of noise. The old lady is being sent to heaven on a memorable tide.

There's a huge queue at the roadside turnstiles. The Bully brothers are hammered. They look at each other and gesture to you.

Follow us, the Older one says.

He jumps on top of a rubbish bin attached to a streetlight four feet away from the wall above the turnstiles. He balances for a second, and to resounding cheers from the queuing fans, jumps the short distance to the top of the wall. Pulls himself up as far as he can, with Younger Bully assisting from below. He does the same, and you push him up by his feet. They jump off the top. Many clubs have walls topped with barbed wire and embedded glass to prevent gatecrashers, but not Notts.

You jump onto the bin and follow them over. It's harder than it looks, and you nearly fall until a passerby pushes you up by the heel. You drop the eight feet down the other side and land safely.

You see that the Bullys are arguing with two stewards.

What are you doing? One says. Sneaking in like this.

Can't be arsed to queue. Do you want the money? Younger Bully says.

I'm kicking you out, says one, a wiry looking jobsworth, pockmarked with a tash and a cap.

Fuck off, Older Bully responds.

The chief steward arrives. You know him, but not well.

You two idiots, he states, flatly.

That's us! They respond.

Let em in, he instructs the two stewards. It's the last game. Repeat this and you're barred.

The three of you work your way through the crush to the stairway leading to the Roadside terraces and seats. At the top, Older Bully spots a Luton fan with a big moon face, a brawny neck and a grey-blouson jacket. He's much older than the three of you and has a Kevin Keegan perm, the first you've seen for a good ten years. Cheekily, he is surreptitiously tripping up Notts fans as they walk past, nudging and elbowing them with a big grin. Older Bully sprints up the stairs, taps him on the shoulder and punches him in his face, sending him reeling. A big bloke, he swiftly recovers and runs back into the seats. Stewards block the exits and egress to the seating area as Luton fans in the Roadside seats begin to come down the stairs towards the scene. Grey jacket is furiously screaming at Older Bully who gives plenty back before merging into the massed ranks, and the whistle goes for kick off

Chapter 10

Saturday. March.

You've arranged to meet some of the lads after the match. It's a long time since you've been in this situation. You're in the TBI, and you have the backroom to yourselves. Notts won 3-1 and maintained their challenge for promotion under Curle. Everyone is in a good mood. Beanie is holding court, telling a few jokes. Spring can be discerned in the air outside. There are more jumpers and light jackets than coats and scarves. Two young lads you don't know are talking to Beanie. The new breed in Burberry jackets and Hackett caps. Smart, neatly turned out, heads shaved like Special Forces. They talk for ages, and they leave with a nod to the old boys who are having a laugh about something. There are girlfriends and wives around - which is a new one on you. That was never encouraged. However, it's a different world, and you wished you had thought to ask Rita. Beanie comes over. You're sitting with Tom and Little Dave.

He pulls up a stool, places a full pint of Snorker's Basket in front of him on the table.

See that lot? He gestures to the departing young lads. They've been on the Internet talking to them pricks from up north that did the Globe two years ago. Apparently, they're coming down next month mob-handed. Sixty of them.

So? Tom comments, nonchalantly.

Well, cheekychops. They want to know whether we can give them a hand.

Not a chance, he says. I'm fifty.

That's what I thought you'd say.

Besides, they can handle it. There's thirty of them.

That's not enough, Tom. They need at least twenty more to give them a fair chance.

Tom says nothing. Sips his beer. Others have gathered round and are listening to Beanie. He continues.

Be a laugh, wouldn't it.

We're too old, Beanie, Tom says drily.

It's just a number, meowd. Age is just a number.

The proposition is discussed for a while, with some keen to get involved, others not sure, and some not bothering.

Later, in the Globe, the subject comes up.

It comes up again in The Bank in town and it comes up again at Lloyds.

Beanie is nothing if not persistent. He is also drunk.

You notice that the people who aren't interested in the occult side of the football experience start to avoid him like the plague.

There are the usual concerns.

Mostly jobs and coppers, the same as in the old days, but overall, the main barrier to getting back on the hooliganism train is age.

Later on, in the Cross Keys - alongside the handsome urban professionals, carefree students and earnest young transmetropolitans sipping bottled WKD's out on the Galleria, the tram in the background transporting pretty pre-loaded teenage girls with heavily lacquered hair and trowelled-on makeup to the Lace Market - the topic of the fight returns to the agenda.

It gets higher up the order of business the more drink is consumed.

It always did. Nothing changes much, really.

You look round. In your opinion, the prospects of getting anyone to join in with Beanies Dad's Army expedition are a bit slim. There are countless barriers.

You stand on your own at the bar. You sip lager and assess the situation.

No one in the room would see forty, Most are overweight by a stone, some by considerably more. One, a character you don't really know, is that obese he can't stand for more than ten minutes unsupported and even during that optimistic burst of activity, he has to find something to lean on to stop the panic attacks.

They're a loveable sight.

Pallid skin developed through too much lager and too many chip suppers. Wobbling jowls with lives of their own. Wrinkles no moisturiser can eradicate. Shadowy bags under bloodshot eyes. Nostril hair as profuse as a rainforest bush. Hairy ears. Head hair at a premium - what there is grows silvery grey. Yellowing crowns, rattling bridges, shifting plates and loose-fitting dentures. Magnificent bellies full of ale that have taken thirty years to cultivate. Kids to consider and despairing menopausal partners.

There is the job situation to consider.

No one in their forties wants to lose a job - not in the middle of a recession. Not when the Jobcentre employs French hatchet men to stop your dole or your sick money. Not when every job you apply for means you're going to be competing with eager Poles and enthusiastic Estonians who would work like beasts of the field for fifty pence an hour as long as they can live in a country with pot noodles, Internet, the best betting infrastructure on the planet and shops where everything costs a pound. Not when every job *you* go for means you are competing with good-looking, liberal, intelligent graduates who shave properly, change their boxer shorts, spend thirty-seven quid on haircuts, go to the gym four nights a week, have all their own teeth and know how to use Power Point.

No. You don't fancy Beanie's rabble-rousing chances at all.

You call Rita on your mobile phone and tell her that you're going to be home later than you thought.

She says it's alright, but you don't believe her. There's something in her voice, something existing below the level of normal perception. You worry that you're being paranoid. You wish she were there with you. You feel uneasy as you put your phone back in your pocket and you decide to drink two more pints maximum, even though the evening excites you and everyone is animated, and it's going to be a good one, just like the endless nights of your twenties. It's amazing to you how little has changed.

Beanie comes up to you. He's slurring and is very, very drunk.

You know what happened to Bacchus, don't you, he asks.

I do, yes.

He goes silent for a bit. There's some garage-style music playing in the pub, which you don't place, but you've heard it come from Perry's bedroom. Beanie leans over you.

That Gordon disappeared. Do you know what happened to the Bully brothers?

I don't, no.

They both packed it in after Luton. Fucking madness. We didn't see much of them after that. I heard one of them works out in Tashkent. He does something with oil wells and that.

Which one?

I don't fucking know. One of them. The other one is...

He tails off. Shakes his head subtly. Takes a sip of his beer... well, you know.

What? You ask, curious. Up until meeting Beanie, you hadn't thought of the Bully brothers for fifteen years.

He's ill. The Older One, I think. Yeh, the older cunt. The one with the fags. I didn't know them that well.

You're kidding. Ill?

That's what Haxford said the other week.

Apparently, he has a year tops.

Cancer?

No, German fucking measles, he said scornfully. You saw the way he got them fags down his neck. And he could drink. His liver must be the size of a chipolata sausage.

Jesus.

No one's seen pair on em for ages.
What happened to that Asif?
The Paki?
Well, yes. Asif.
Dunno. He just stopped coming.

It didn't help that everyone apart from the Bully brothers treated him like shit, you think, but you don't say that because it's a little bit too controversial to discuss when everyone is at least, ten pints up. The whole incident wasn't one of Notts' finer moments. You didn't know him that well, but you know no one really stuck up for him or made him feel welcome. You know you didn't.

And he loved Notts.
Absolutely loved the club.
Are you coming back against the Northern raiders? Beanie asks, climatically. A serious look on his face.
He's expecting a positive answer.
I don't know, mate. I don't know. It's been a long, long time.
Be a devil. Go on. England expects and all that...
I'll think about it.
You can even wear your gear.
You laugh. You haven't thought about sportswear for years. Some of them kids can lend me a Burberry cap, Beanie. I can't afford gear like that - not with Perry and the missus.
I'll see what I can do. In our heyday, we'd have hammered them cunts.
I know.
They were nothing back then.
He's drunk and getting maudlin. You're starting to feel uncomfortable.
Yes, you reply.
We took our eye off the ball, youth. We should have carried on.
Why?

Come here. He taps you on the shoulder, and you follow him outside. You ever had a look at this place?

What, the tram?

No, Nottingham. Tahn. Ey a look.

You don't need to look. You know these streets intimately. You see the regenerated Lace Market. The Contemporary Art Museum, which had so recently displayed Hockney and a retrospective of the Pre-Raphaelites. The Pitcher and Piano pub-in-a-Church. You see the tram and the rejuvenated bars with trendy names like Ha Ha on the other side of the tramlines, which stretch all the way up to Hockley, full of happy revellers.

I work here, you say.

I know you do, wankstain. Have you ever had a *look,* I mean. A real good *gander* at the state we live in. Look behind the money, youth. Look behind the obvious.

Sometimes, you reply. Not often.

He's starting to slur his words. Beanie was never like this when we were younger. Something is definitely getting under his skin. You've noticed in the pub, lately.

Maybe it's being out of work. You've always been a good listener. You carry on listening, even though you'd rather be talking about something else, and listening to the Snow Patrol track coming from inside the Keys. All these fellas in Keys. I love em. I do. They live for Notts, and so do I, but what's the point? What's the difference between us and someone who goes Ice Skating down there? Beanie points in the general direction of the Nottingham Arena. He drains his bottle of WKD and walks to the window, taps on it. Dave nods and goes to the bar for another.

Nowt. There IS no fucking difference. Planting bulbs. Mowing lawn. Skating a pirouette. Going to flicks. Watching Notts. None of it means fuck all. At least with scrapping, there was a *point* to it.

Was there? You say, not convinced. A point?

Yes, there was bollocks. Hooliganism, that wasn't just a hobby, a pastime, it was *a way of life!* Men need a hobby to take their minds of the *mundanimity* of existence, I'm not telling you owt you don't know there, being an intelligent man and a bloke to boot, but it takes a rare bird to follow something as a *way of life*, a culture. It takes bottle to pack it all in to enrol at a Shaolin temple, or sail to Africa to help starving Somalis in camps a hundred thousand strong. It takes real moxeh to stop the Japs butchering every whale in the Antarctic by getting in the road of the whaling ships on a Greenpeace boat. Handing over all your worldly goods to chariteh and go wandering the world, throwing yourself in front of some rain forest destroying bulldozer in Brazil. Helping resurrect the North American Bison that we wiped out in first place. That's bottle. God, I wish I ed the bottle to do sumut like that.

He winks at you and leans closer, switches topic.

Watching football without fighting is like window shopping at Harrods, matey.

Little Dave appears with a luminous bottle of blue WKD. Beanie hugs him. He looks embarrassed.

We're off up The Approach in a bit, Beanie, he says.

That's a right Forest shithole, that is, Beanie replies, swaying, nearly spilling the drink as he collects it.

I don't make the choices, Little Dave says. See him if you have any complaints - Dave gestures over his shoulder at Haxford, holding court inside. Beanie laughs and takes a big guzzle. He's skipping from one topic to another incoherently, expecting you to put the pieces together if there is an end product to this. His rant is sobering you up, and you're glad about that.

At least, we go to games. Not like them plastic shagnasties who watch Sky Sports and buy Man Utd replica shirts. I watched this documentareh the other day. They were interviewing some Malaysian Manure fans. Out there. In Kuala Lumpur. One of them was complaining about a loss to Norwich, or some Muppet Prem team like that, I forget which. He says, *'it'll be different when we get them back to our patch!'* I pissed myself laughing. Then I realised there are people *in this countreh* who have never *seen* Old Trafford, and yet they *support Man Utd!* *'Our patch'*. Unbelievable. Unfuckingbelievable.

I think you're rambling a bit now, Beanie.

It all makes *perfect* sense to me, mate.

What's your point, then?

My point, dear sir, he says drunkenly as he airily gestures to the night sky, is that YOU need to turn up next month.

I thought we'd changed the subject, you say.

We *ALL* need to turn up next month because life has no point otherwise, youth. Look at that lot. Look at you. Look at little moi. Look at these posh wankstains with the puff's cocktails here, he says loudly, gesturing at the trendy students and call centre executives on the Galleria enjoying intelligent conversation in mostly mixed racial and gender-based groups. A young man with a casual just out of bed haircut that probably took him an hour under a hairdryer to achieve turns round and gives Beanie a quizzical look. Then he looks at his drink, which is indeed, a brightly-coloured cocktail full of crushed ice and crimson syrup.

The girl he's with stares at Beanie coldly.

Look at them all, he continues. They go to work. Them that ey jobs, that is. Fuck me, it's a living hell for those that ain't. They come home. Eat tea and fall asleep on their favourite armchair. Watch soaps or Strictly Come Dancing. Cooking shows with Jamie Oliver, or Cash in the Attic, or Homes under the Hammer, or Bargain Hunt, or reality shows about American housewives. They lose the inheritance on Internet Poker. Go out and play five-a-side with their fat mates at the Leisure Centre. Chat up old girlfriends on Facebook. Surf the net for photos of insecure teenage birds taking photos of themsens naked in bedroom mirrors. Snack on cupcakes at a quid a pop, or four packs of blueberry muffins until they become a health statistic for the NHS five-a-day fascists. The lucky ones get to shag their wives, those that have em: The *really* lucky ones might even enjoy it. Every day is the same shit. Every Saturday, they have a lie in. Get hammered round here at night. Hungover, they go for a pint and a game of brag Sunday dinner in the Rose and Crown, and they fall asleep on the sofa while the missus cooks the roast. They sit round with the kids on Sunday night seeing which talent-starved nobodeh is kicked off X-Factor, and they lie in bed weeping like little girls because it's work tomorrow, and they fucking hate it. Absolutely hate every second of it. The eternal traffic jams, the dull people they have to wok wi, the managers who make them beg for treats like abused dogs in an RSPCA sanctuary, the ever-present threat of redundancy hanging over them like fucking mustard gas. It all kicks off, day in, day out, day in, day out, with the exception of that traumatic fortnight in Benidorm, and even more traumatic week off at Christmas, with kids who once loved you, and now couldn't give a fuck whether you lived or died.

He gestures grandly and staggers a little.

This little scenario, with obvious variations, mate, is repeated a quarter of a million times in Nottingham. And do you know what it is?

What?

Do you know what it all is?

I don't, Beanie. No, I don't.

A suicide note in daily parts, youth.

He points a finger at your heart and taps it lightly with his fingertip. He leans toward you until you can smell his aftershave and see his heavily-lidded eyes up close.

You really need to front the Northerners, buddy. It'll give your life some *purpose.*

Will it, you reply.

One thing's for sure. It'll put some colour back into them chubby *cheeks*.

Beanie pinches your right cheek until you wince and grins at you. Puts the bottle of WKD down and wanders off somewhere, leaving you alone with your thoughts. You hide your pint on a table in the middle of the throng of metrosexuals outside the window, and you stand at the wall, waiting for your old friends to walk down to the Approach.

When you get home, Rita isn't in.

Perry is asleep. You call Rita, but she's switched her phone off. It's two in the morning, so you don't want to call her sister. You know she's not there. She must have gone into town. You're too drunk to ponder and sift the implications. You turn the laptop on and listen to The Farm, Altogether Now. Soon, you're fast asleep on the sofa, fully clothed.

Rita never told you where she was that night, and you never asked.

They say you should never ask a question unless you already know the answer. Only ask a question, if you are prepared for an answer you might not want to hear.

On this occasion, you neither know the answer to the question, nor do you want to hear it.

She was in bed when you woke up, everything normal, and she never said anything about it the following day. She was her normal, quiet self. She spent the day cooking a roast, listening to dance music on Radio One Extra. She talked to you about work. If anything, her temporary disappearance seemed to you a symbol of something, rather than anything real. At least she was still *there*. You could still see her pottering around the kitchen. You could smell her perfume. You could hear her chatting away about nothing. You could hear her hum her kitchen songs. You could see her look out the window on tiptoe, sipping a mug of coffee, watching the Finches nibbling seed on the bird table.

You could see her coffee-coloured legs in denim shorts wandering round the house. She was still there, even though she hardly ever looks at you nowadays and she never, ever uses your name in conversation.

She was still *there*.

You both fell asleep after dinner, and in the evening, the two of you sat down with Perry.

You watched Countryfile, a preview of Britain's Got Talent, Coronation Street, Jamie Oliver's Britain, That's Britain, half of Heartbeat (but not with that Nick Berry); a bit of John Bishop's Britain, and all of Strictly Celebrity Apprentice Detective Loose Antique Estate Agent Women Karaoke Masterchef in the Jungle before crying yourself to sleep, alone, thinking about how much you hate your job and wishing Rita would love you like she used to.

All Good Things

Final whistle. The fans flood the pitch, the stewards and coppers unable to hold back the tsunami.

It's 2-1. Notts. Luton relegated to the second tier. The pitch is full, the traditional end of season celebration. You remember being a kid, Cardiff, where it all started. The police are holding back the hordes of Luton, some of whom are climbing the away fences. Grey jacket comes from out of the skies and punches Older Bully in the back of the head. He doesn't see it coming and falls to the floor. You hit the Luton fan, a glancing blow, and another punch, coming from behind you, connects with his nose like an Exocet. Bloodied, Grey jacket falls to the floor, but he's soon up, his contorted face a whirlwind of rage. Stewards come from everywhere and surround him, a dazed Older Bully, too. It looks all over for him, all the fun to come. Some guardian angel in a cap tells the chief steward what he saw, and the finger of suspicion firmly points at Luton, who after some debate about cause and effect, is carted off by two smirking coppers. A grateful Bully seizes the moment and skips onto the pitch, disappears into the melee. Sporadic outbreaks of fighting occur in the stands, on the terraces and on the pitch. The stewards and the cops are busy, and it has not even reached the streets yet. The tannoyman thanks those present for their support, repeatedly, like a three-minute warning. The atmosphere is nasty, about to go nuclear, no time to grieve the passing of Old Meadow Lane and its firetrap stands, its chipped and broken terracing, its debris-strewn ruins.

There's no time for contemplation and no time for grieving because it's every man for himself and the four thousand Luton penned in the Kop are ready to be released from their metal cages, frothing at the mouth like rabid dogs. You jump over the side, see a MIG in a Navy Blue Ellesse squash shirt looking menacingly at three young shirters. You creep up behind him, tap him on the shoulder, say hey, mate, have you got the time, then headbutt him on the bridge of his nose. He's dazed, struggling to get back off the ground before the three count. A civilian you don't recognise weighs in with a boot in his chin and even a kid, no older than ten, sticks an Adidas Samba into his ribs. You rub your forehead because the Glasgow Kiss is a double-edged sword and for a moment, you notice the Lane End spin and blur. Tom taps *you* on the shoulder, and the two of you run toward Meadow Lane. Outside, civilians scatter, an unnatural space developing outside the Meadow Club.

Families make haste. You hear a dad tell his wife and kid to walk up toward the Magpies pub, away from the carnage. He runs back into the space as if he's doing something noble. There is a coach - the away team coach in the middle of the road, and you see a brick go through the windscreen. The noise is incredible, an urban riot spawned in rage, frustration, disappointment, but most of all, culture and tradition. It's out with the old, in with new, on the last game of the season, the old Saturday afternoons passing by, ready for thirty-eight more Saturday afternoons being prepared for next season, the whole of the summer to heal wounds and rebuild the destruction. There's fighting all over the road. Not just lads. It seems everyone is up for it. You and Tom trot over to the Meadow Club and see what's developed. Nearest the road, there's thirty Luton, who've clearly left the ground early for a few pints. MIGS. Holding a Union Jack with Luton FC written on it in big white letters. Notts are playing Capture the Flag, charging the MIGS to try and steal it, but the Luton are fighting like lions, outnumbered for the time being, the main body of the Luton hordes being held back. There's no quarter given in the ruck. Tornado fists connect in a flurry. Mechanical boots go in on the prone. Your priority is to stay on your feet because if you go down, you're history. You run in and land the sole of your trainer in the chest of someone with a smart-blonde wedge, who looks like Nick

Heyward from Haircut One Hundred. He swings back. You feel a thud and know you've been hit on the shoulder with a stone or a brick. You wince. Someone calls you a Northern cunt and before you can say, no, get it right, I'm from *The Midlands,* he smacks you in the cheek - a good one, he's wearing a signet ring and you feel a tooth go. Someone else punches you, poor sod, a cat in a washing machine full of punches, and you and Stuart are in the middle of an almighty scrum where it's difficult to know who is Notts and who's a MIG.

You hit one, two, three people and you see one go down underfoot, a dangerous place to be in a melee like this, and you're down as you're nutted on the cheek by a bloke in a sky-blue tracksuit top (which you admire, and make a mental note to look up the next time you're down on the Portobello Road). He's taken three Notts out in no time at all. You look up, Notts have the Luton flag and are running back toward the Meadow Club, and the enraged MIGS go after it. On the road, you see Younger Bully escorted by three burly coppers, kicking and screaming past the coach, a familiar sight, blood pouring down his cheek. He looks like he's been slashed. You see the MIGS regain the standard and you get up, run five yards and jump on the flag carrier, and you both fall to the floor. Suddenly, it goes dark, the flurry of trainers and boots hitting you (but you're been there before, and it doesn't hurt you, does it, *does* it), but it's no good, your arm is taking a battering, someone stamps on your hand, and you let go of the flag.

The groups separate. Exhausted, but elated, you see two Black Marias come from nowhere, coppers in hi-vis jackets pouring out the back. You run with the rest into the Meadow Club, desperate not to get pulled. Someone you half recognise comes toward you as you walk through the door. You're about to say hello when he punches you in the eye, and it's a big punch, an Ali, a Frasier, a Holmes, a Benn, and you're sparked on the carpet. You hear someone tell the man that you're Notts and to leave it out. Turns out he's a Calverton Sunderland fan who goes away with the Notts England lot. Out for a pint with the boys. He thought you were Luton. He bends down and apologises. Couldn't be nicer about it.

Sorry, mate. I'm sorry about that.

You laugh. It's funny when you think about it. All of it. All of it is hysterical. Saturday afternoon entertainment for the working classes. You shake hands. You get up and lean on a stanchion because you've taken a good one there, a real purler.

The doors of the club shut. Outside, the coppers surround the MIGS who still have the flag. They can't move. Most Notts are back inside, and the civilians begin to move outside in both directions. It's mostly Luton outside, on the way to the coaches. Older Bully is moaning, trying to get out, but the bouncers won't let him out of the club. *They've nicked our kid! They've nicked our kid!* You can't talk to him when he's like that, but Tom tries, pulls him away from the door. The hubbub and buzz is intense, almost as intense as the fighting itself. Everyone's talking about it, one of the best battles at Meadow Lane ever, a non-stop orgy of ultra violence.

You hear about how Younger Bully got nicked from Bacchus and Gordon.

Lots of others chip in.

Turns out Younger Bully had carried out one of his one-man suicide missions behind the Roadside, a walk of death, down the centre of the road, drifting to one side, then back to the other, merging with the crowds, demerging at warp speed, punching, kicking, nutting, kneeing, booting, screaming, screaming, screaming, total and complete random ultra violence straight out of a book or a film.

He had made quite an impression on the breathless onlookers who queued up to tell anyone who would listen what they saw. The words and stories form an impression, but you're out of breath and dazed. The details don't sink in. You've been kicked to hell and back. You've received three decent punches, particularly the one spawned in the North East. They all counted, and your head hurts. You know you're going to have a black eye, a bad one. Older Bully is listening, a proud elder brother. The whole become a torrent of urban snippets, like a fable dissected and shared out among novice storytellers.

Oh, man, he hit every bastard. Anyone who looked like a fucking MIG...

...took three on, the mad bastard. Then another.

...waited for um to leave Kop. Ambushed em on is own...

...went down like a felled tree...

...ran off like little girls...

...Incredible performance off the pitch...

...best of the season. Best ever if you ask me...

...Amazing. Fucking amazing. He's insane, that cunt...

...the bloke will go down for that. He cracked one, then another, and another. I saw him run up to this geezer with a gob on him and hit him with a right. I reckon he's still dahn nah...

...nutted the cunt, blood everywhere...

...If it had a fucking cockney accent, he took the fucker aht. Ne'er seen owt like it...

Older Bully, listening to this, decides enough is enough, and you don't know why, maybe you're still dazed and confused, but you follow him. This time, the bouncers let you out into the empty street, the coppers in full control. Older Bully trots down the lane toward the Main Stand where the cells are. You follow, turn into the Main Stand. You see a copper up ahead without his helmet. Older Bully goes up to him to ask about his brother, but next thing you know, there's the dead hand of the law on his shoulder, and he's being marched to the cells.

Another copper, as if from nowhere, grabs hold of you roughly.

We've been a bit naughty today, haven't we? Time for Naughty Corner with the other idiots, he says and marches you to the cells.

Neither of you struggle. There is no point when you've reached this stage. You may as well take your medicine like a good boy.

The cops throw the two of you into the same cell as Younger Bully.

There are others in other cells, and you can hear people shouting - Luton, by the sounds - but the three of you are in the cell on your own.

What a waste of valuable drinking time this is, the younger brother says.

They won't keep us long, Older Bully says. You've been a bit naughty, I hear.

Luton get on my tits. Gave us the runaround last year, remember?

I do.

You're a bit of a hero, Older Bully says, rubbing his brother's hair.

No one gave me a hand. Shitters.

To be fair, he replies. I wouldn't give you a hand when you're in that mood.

Younger Bully nods. Lies down on the seats, bare-chested, his tee-shirt a pillow.

You might get put down for that, youth, his brother offers shortly after.

Who gives a fuck, comes the reply.

You remain in the cells for two hours. Maybe it's the drink, or the impact of the Sunderland punch (which still throbs), but you decide to ask the Bullys their names.

They had been silent for an hour, deep in their own thoughts. It's an opportune moment.

You sit next to Older Bully.

What's your first name? You ask. I get sick of thinking of you as Older Bully.

You smile. The request couldn't have been softer and more accommodating. A technique you learned on a sales course in Kidderminster. Soften the scenario. Make it unthreatening. They're bound to tell you - you're sharing a common crisis together.

The three of you are sharing an *ordeal.*

He sits there, bites a fingernail.

Younger Bully, who has been sleeping drunkenly, wakes up, sits up and puts on the shirt. He's heard the question.

His face is impassive, the scar underneath his right eye unmoving, his eyes and lips still.

You're worried,

You don't know whether you've done the wrong thing.

You wish you could turn back the clock. Five seasons of perfect social development. Understanding of male social groups. Textbook. The hierarchies. The compartmentalised identities. The rituals, and the rules, the dos and don'ts. All potentially ruined by one daft question born out of curiosity. Neither of them says anything. Then they look at each other. It seems like a psychic telegram passes between them.

Bully, says the older one. That's my name. Bully.

Me, too. I'm Bully, says the younger one.

We have no other names, the older one says, flatly.

There are only the Bully brothers, says the younger one. Simultaneously, they wink at you.

Anyway, the older one asks, conspiratorially, leaning over toward you, so close that you can smell the rancid lunchtime Stella on his breath.

Never mind *us* ...

...What's *your* name?

The door opens, and a smiling copper with a moustache, which makes him look like Dickie Davies, is waiting for you and the Bully brothers.

You get yourselves together and walk outside to the temporary custody desk. Behind the desk sits the Assistant Chief Constable. Grey haired and hawk-nosed, a pair of silver spectacles. He's not smiling.

He tells you that you're free to go without charge.

Then he looks at the brothers.

You two idiots have been causing problems down here for a decade.

We...

Shut it and listen. I've had enough. I've checked your charge sheets, and they make grim reading. You are Category A hooligans. How you have made it this far without a stretch, I don't know. I tell you now, it stops. Do you hear me? It stops. If I catch you engaged in misbehaviour down here, you're going straight to prison. No magistrate's court. No bail. No conditional discharges or community service. None of that bollocks. You'll be eating porridge for breakfast for six months. I mean it. I'm not kidding. The fun is over at Notts County for you two idiots. Do you understand?

The brothers both nod. Standing next to them, you are stunned at the cold steel behind his proclamation, and despite the questionable legality, you are in no doubt that he means what he says.

Now, piss off, he concludes and the three of you walk out into the late evening sunshine.

Haxford and the gang are waiting outside the Main Stand gates.

You are greeted with handshakes. Haxford walks up to Younger Bully and shakes his.

We're going out for a good drink, he says. Fun's over, Bully. Let's see how much drink we can drink and how many women blow out Sea Monster. Coppers are still everywhere. Let's leave it for nah. Haxford is at least ten years older than Younger Bully and much more experienced. He's been warned twice in five minutes. Haxford hates fighting in pubs and sees Saturday nights as a social end to the week. The younger man nods quietly. He sees a Skoda Estelle parked alone on the side of the road. An inoffensive car painted a sickly mixture of amber and lemon. It's old and forlorn, sad, a car even its current owners probably don't want. A Muscovite would disown it. Its student owners had probably abandoned it. He looks round to see if there are any coppers. He looks at Haxford.

Winks.

Runs over to the car, jumps on the boot and smashes the rear window. To hoots and laughter from everyone except Haxford, he dents the roof, slides down and puts the windscreen through.

He dismounts the car and walks off towards Trent Bridge.

That told me, says Haxford. Crazy Bastard.

There's about fifteen of you, drunk and looking forward to getting drunker. It's getting dark rapidly, but there is still a trace of setting sun in the sky, a flash of crimson red embedded in ambient orange.

Trent Bridge is busy with cars and Saturday night revellers on their way to the Aviary. Up ahead, you see lads outside the café and instinctively, you know they're unfriendly. Everyone runs towards them spontaneously, unprompted and most of the enemy make a run for it. Three or four stand their ground. They take a beating because there is no way tonight Notts are going to lose on a crest of the wave, but it's not a bad beating, and you allow them to get up and run back toward their van in the TBI car park.

The majority aren't MIGS, more like suburban Luton on a stag do, but the lads who stood were definitely football. You let them get into the van, and you walk into the TBI, the pub on the boundary of the Trent

Bridge Cricket Ground. The bouncers let you in, which means there are no Luton. At the bar are three Notts players and most of the lads go over to say hello. Notts' six hundred thousand pound record buy, Antonio Aggriana, in demand centre back Derek Yeast, and someone you don't recognise. A youth player. On a table in the lounge sit some Forest players. One of whom is Danny Eager, the combatative midfielder, and you recognise Liam Wayne.

The Bully brothers despise Forest and rather than go to mix with the Notts players, they sit down with the smartly-dressed Forest pair. The bouncers walk over and watch the situation develop. Clarkson and Tomjoin, the Bullies and you stand at the wall.

There are two social situations developing here, one friendly and one anything but.

Eager isn't giving an inch and is staring Younger Bully out. Wayne tries to buy everyone a drink in that chirpy Scouse way of his, but Younger Bully and Eager are at it and nothing is going to get in the way of that.

You hear Bully call Eager a Forest bastard.

Eager just stares, says nothing.

It's like something out of the old west.

Are you insulting my mule?

If I were you, I'd get out of Tombstone on the next stage.

Pick up the gun. Go on...pick up the gun...

You going to pull them pistol or whistle Dixie...

It seems to you as if everything is suspended in time, a scenario framed in a glass bottle. Antonio Aggriana comes over and tries to be diplomatic.

You work out the odds.

Younger Bully is twice the size of Eager, but a quarter as fit. Beanie comes over and offers you evens, each of two, but you don't know what he's talking about. Now Derek Yeast comes over, football players generally knowing no tribal loyalties, playing for the highest bidder and mixing with the enemy, and he stands between the two. Leave it out, come on, let's have a drink. He's impeccably dressed, and you can tell he genuinely wants to talk about football with football fans.

It's just a pity that tonight he'd met the wrong crowd, most of whom couldn't tell you who played today because they don't really give a toss about the minutae.

While you're thinking this, something clicks, something snaps, and Younger Bully lets rip a snake-like punch, which hits Eager in the face and the Forest man throws one back with a snarl and the whole place is round the table, a mass of bodies. Bouncers jump on Younger Bully and drag him expertly out of the pub. Eager sits down, and you can tell he's shocked. Wayne is trying to stop the rest of the Notts steam into the dislikeable Eager, and Aggriana and Yeast form a protective barrier while the bouncers go to work.

You slip out quietly, not really having been part of it. It's dark outside and one-by-one, Notts are ejected, Haxford arguing with the head bouncer, trying desperately to get a refund for the four pints he'd just paid for without taking a single sip.

You know there is no chance of a pint in The Aviary as they are all the same firm of bouncers and the walkie-talkies would be crackling away.

Haxford is not amused. Let's go back to the Meadow and tahn, he says. That's it, Bully. Enough nah. Stop fucking hitting people! He says, and he means it and Younger Bully nods and says okay, which could mean anything.

Breaker, Stuart and Clarkson return from chasing five Luton down Radcliffe Road and talk about it animatedly.

It starts to fragment, with the drink and the differing motivations, assembled needs splitting.

You start to feel flat. You've had half a pint in three hours, and you need one to get yourself back in the groove.

You hear the Meadow Club mentioned, and everyone walks back over the Bridge to the City side, away from Rushcliffe.

You look over the side of the bridge into the depths of the black river. Lights skirt the banks. Concentric ripples flow away from an insubstantial radial point, breaking abruptly on the steps. Other competing ripples fade into nothingness before developing a head of steam.

A pleasure boat floats past, full of revellers enjoying their Saturday night after a hard week at work. You watch them in their expensive dresses and their stiletto heels, their bowties and their black tuxedos.

These are Nottingham's beautiful people.

The cameramen from the Nottingham Topic will be there, on the Poop Deck, on the Captain's Table, snapping away, recording the frivolity of the rich for posterity and the delectation of the masses.

A string quartet plays something beguiling at the prow of the boat. Couples in love dance slowly. Against the background of the traffic crossing over Trent Bridge, you can hear snippets of conversation, grainy laughter and the clink of champagne flutes as the boat sails past into the distance, creating yet more ephemeral ripples, condemned to fade away before they have even been created.

You realise you're lagging behind the rest and you trot to catch up. The gang take the shortcut through Turney's Quay and onto Meadow Lane for the second time that day.

The alley is six foot across.

Scene of a terrifying fight versus Tottenham when you were young.

Nowhere to run.

Nowhere to hide.

If you get caught in the alley, you HAVE to fight.

You walk down in a line, no more than fifty feet long, heading toward the Navigation pub. Someone whispers.

Lads! Up ahead!

As if life had become an exact mirror image, fifteen men turn the corner and are now walking up the alley, hugging the wall on the other side.

There's perhaps, room for four across in this alley, and you know this is going to get very tasty, very quickly.

You tense and clench your fist, and you sense the others do the same.

This is going to be the best yet, the worst yet; mass mayhem. There's no space and nowhere to run. Six feet across.

One person walking up.

One person walking down.

Suddenly everything becomes an imp in the silvered glass, a mirrored phantom flickering in the darkness.

They slow down. You slow down.
They go silent. You go silent.
Still you walk. Still they walk.
You have no idea who they are.
They could be Notts.
They could be Luton.

The alley is unlit and the moon is obscured by drifting clouds. It's near pitch dark. You see someone opposite you, but you can't see his face.

You sense them rather than see them.
Doppelgangers.
Ephemeral, mirrored presence, the scent of testosterone.
The news gets passed back in whispers.
Someone recognises them.

Forest.

It's *Forest*.

They walk alongside like ships in the night.
You attune to the darkness and recognise some of them.
Forest top lads.
You can't remember where they've been today, but they've obviously come down for a sniff about.
You can't sense a psychic consensus about what to do.
(Do we hit? Do we run?)
All of a sudden, there are no leaders.
They stop. You stop.
They turn and face you.
You turn and face them.
Equal numbers, but no consensus.
Some will want to fight.
Some will want to run.
Some like Forest.
Some hate Forest.
You hear a couple of heyups down the line.
It's a small city.
There's not much mixing, but there's a lot of cohabitation.
Not much choice, really.
Not if you don't want a massacre every night in your own city.

You look down the line and see the Bully brothers.
You see Haxford.
You see Jules.
You see Clarkson.
You see Preece.
You see Beanie.
You see Breaker.
You see Little Dave.
You see Tom, and The Printer, and Paul.
You see Stuart.

You have no idea how this is going to turn out.
You fight here, and that's the end of the détente.
Every night out in Nottingham will end in bloodshed.

No more Fountain.
No more Dog and Bear.
No more Arriba Club.
No more good times.

Forest outnumber Notts five to one.
You are an ethnic minority in your own city.

Even on a good day, you can muster fifty to sixty lads for an important fixture.
Forest can make two hundred even for a distance trip to Portsmouth or Newcastle. Notts would be lucky to make thirty.
Every bad boy in Nottingham, from Bulwell to Broxtowe, from Clifton to Top Valley, and all the ancient mining and mill towns skirting the A610 - the Ripleys, the Heanors, the Langley Mills, the Eastwoods, the Ilkestons, even the suburbs and pit towns as far north as Calverton and Hucknall, and Newark and Mansfield, they all follow Forest.

That's Clough's real legacy.
Not Europe.
Not the late seventies trophy cabinet.
Local tribal expansion.

At one time, there were equal numbers.
Five to one.
Notts.
Ethnically cleansed.
The Genocide of the Colonial Masters.
The visit of Columbus to Hispaniola.

Clough.
Columbus.

The Extinction of the Tiano.
The Trail of Tears.
They know this.
They stare at you, and they know.
They *know*.

You are the Last of the Magpies.
They know this.
Your oppressors wait patiently over the other side of the alley. No words are necessary.
It's kill or be killed, now or never.

But they can feel it.
They can feel something.
You've been fighting all day, and they haven't.
Blood's up.
You've no fear.
Knuckles hardened. They can see the bruises on your face and the bloodstains on your shirts.
You don't give a shit whether you live or die.
It's the hunt, the kill.

You are veterans of the May slaying.
A mental advantage that *just might* give you the edge.
You wonder what Beanie's odds are for this match.
There is silence and stillness.
You wait.
Nothing moves for the longest time.
You look down the line.

Haxford gestures toward the Navigation and Notts slowly start to walk. The mirror image over the other side of the wall walks in the opposite direction.

There are no words.
You drink in the Meadow Club.
Then you drink in town.
You meet Rita in the Fountain.
She makes a fuss of your battered face.

Those that still stand go to the Arriba Club.

You and Rita dance.
To anything and everything.

In the taxi home, you tell her that you're at the end.
You're going out on top.
It's all over.
The fighting, the drinking.
Your youth.

She tells you she loves you, and you hold her as the sun begins to rise over Mansfield Road.

Epilogue

Sitting in McDonalds, eating a Bacon and Egg McMuffin. With a small coffee. Town is an unbroken mass of shoppers and you find yourself questioning the recession. There are thousands of people walking up and down Bridlesmith Gate, shopping this Saturday. The pavements sizzle in the sunshine, eighty degrees and counting. It's eleven a.m. More evidence of the global warming that will finish off the human race before long because the Indonesians, and the Brazilians, and the Malaysians won't stop chopping down the trees that keep us alive.

It's more like old school August than April. The shoppers wear shorts and sunglasses, and tee-shirts with ironic slogans and flip flops, and they chat on Blackberries and escape the heat by ducking into air conditioned sports shops to buy more tee-shirts, and shorts, and trainers.

Usually, in the week, Nottingham is one of the most ethnically diverse places you can imagine, with at least three hundred and fifty ethnic and religious groups living within a square mile of the city, but on Saturdays, it's old school, locals, the voracious British locust shopping instinct alive and kicking on Bridlesmith Gate, the fourth trendiest street in the entire country. Something about that sentence makes you feel proud, yet you know it's absurd. You're careful with your Muffin because you're wearing a plain white polo shirt and you don't want to splatter it with tomato ketchup or egg yolk. That could ruin everything. Ray Ban sunglasses are perched on your head.

You're wearing blue jeans you paid a hundred and twenty quid for yesterday, made in Brighton by a firm of ecologically sound clothes gurus. Jeans, which have been nowhere near a Mongolian sweatshop staffed by North Korean slaves. Trainers were harder to find, most modern trainers being hideously ugly, and stitched with the endless tears of Asian children. You declined that mission and pulled out a pair of German-made bordeaux and cerulean Gazelles you brought ten years ago and stored away in the wardrobe. You picked them up on the Internet for a song, and you've always liked them, even if they are a bit Villa.

You're wearing some JPG aftershave and your best wristwatch.

You haven't felt as good as this in years.

You don't know why you feel so good.

You shouldn't do. You should feel the polar opposite.

You have your iPod tucked away in your side pocket. It's your old iPod, the size of the inner sleeve in a packet of ten cigarettes. You haven't played this in years, but it fits. All the old songs are on there. You take it out of your pocket and look at the bands.

Heaven 17. Haircut 100. Happy Mondays. Primal Scream. Stone Roses. Prodigy.

You're listening to *Love Plus One.*

You haven't heard this in years. It reminds you of much better times.

Carefree times.

Inspiral Carpets. The Charlatans. Cocteau Twins. Adamski. Seal. Stereo MC's. Suede.

The iPod selects a funk record.

One Nation Under A Groove.

James. Suede. New Order. The Beloved. Moby. The Farm. The LA's.

You have a punk playlist on there. Sex Pistols. The Clash. Ruts - *Babylon's Burning*, the best punk song ever. Buzzcocks. Banshees.

It had been years since you played this kind of stuff. You forget how much music you actually listened to back in the day. You put the iPod away.

You get a text message. It's Beanie. He tells you where he is, and you text back to tell him you'll be seeing him. You finish your muffin, leave most of your coffee and step out into the sunshine.

They shut the Fountain.
It's been shut for years.
It's a clothes shop catering for the Park Set.
The Dog and Bear is a chocolate shop or something.
The QEII, an undeveloped mess.
The Arriba moved to St James Street.
There are hardly any football pubs left in Nottingham.
Not by comparison. The tourist traps like The Bell, plenty of compact and bijou wine gaffs, alcohol-free coffee bars straight out of Clockwork Orange, hundreds of them, the new meeting places.

You've got your WB Yeats, your Melbourne Inns, your Jug and Sticks, your Magic Spoons and the rest of them, skirted by smokers huddled in the doorways, roll ups in hand, but these are identityless replicas, not real pubs, with managers instead of landlords and the ever present stink of lamb shank vacuum packed two years ago in some Immingham container port, soup of the day straight out of a megatin canned in 2009, somewhere near Toronto. You don't want to seem like an old bastard, but you consider it unavoidable.

Nobody drinks any more, it seems.

You can even remember the days when they built the Vic Centre and included *two pubs in the design, plus one on the outside!*

Pubs in shopping malls. Your dad's brewery got the contract to supply beer. Hard to believe, but it was the norm.

They used to call it Fun City. You read **Hoods** a while back, like everyone else in Nottingham, and the author blames cocaine and ecstasy for the death of Fun City. You'd given it up by then, the drinking and the partying, and the fighting. You'd settled down with Rita and Perry, a life of domestic bliss you loved as you loved her, so you don't know for sure whether he's right or not, in his analysis. He paints a picture of drugs eating away at the fabric of Nottingham like rust devouring metal. You don't know. All you know is between Luton and now, fifteen years later, something changed

Something changed.

All the old pubs have gone.

Beanie has arranged to meet you in the usual place. It's 11.30 a.m. He's downstairs, drinking on his own, just him, the gargoyle and the draught. You fear the worst as he shakes hands, feel a tremble in his wrist and fingers. He's been out last night, and he's struggling to get the beer down. He looks terrible. Pallid. Blotchy. He's wearing a denim shirt and brown Caterpillar boots. He's put a lot of weight on since the pair of you reunited and his belly hangs over his stomach. God knows where he's getting his money.

He tells you that he's just won fifty sovs on a white jacket at Crayford, and that will see him through until at least five. Pay for his match ticket.

There's one answer to the question, you think.

How's Reet? He asks.

Fine. Fine and dandy, you reply.

You wonder whether he feels guilty or not. In the old days, you'd never ask a question like that. You never discussed anything personal. You realised the other day that everything had gone to shit since you bumped into Beanie before Christmas. Sometimes, on the black nights, you blame him for everything. Other times, you don't.

You're well over forty, and you have nothing but your memories.

She been in touch? He asks.

Not since Wednesday. She was perfectly polite, and it was all very amicable, you lied.

Easily.

Still staying at her sister's?

As far as I know. She wants to come home. Only, she wants me not to be there when she does.

Sorry, mate.

Don't be, you reply. It's been coming for a long time. I've lived with it every day.

Okay.

We'll work it out, you lie, take a sip of your lager. It's beautifully cold and tasty with no afterburn and no hint of washing up liquid. One good thing about the modern pub - you may pay three and a half quid for a pint, but it's usually worth it. The beer is usually flawless, unlike the toxic slops they served back in the day.

How's Perry?

Bearing up under the strain. It's quiet today. Where is everyone? I say, trying to change the subject.

I dunno, youth. They made promises.

Where are the kids?

Down in the Magic Spoons in the Square. They keep texting me.

How long do we have? I ask.

Beanie looks at his wristwatch. An hour. Time for another pint. Struggling with this fucker. Spent the night on the White Lightning with the missus watching the *Crank* double bill. Fucking ace films, but I must have ate sumut dodgeh. My guts hurt.

You drain your pint in one. You tell Beanie to hang on, and you stand by the bookshelves.

It's about time.

You look round, and you probe with your fingers while the gargoyle watches on.

You check all the shelves inside and out, pulling out the fake book spines as you go, but there is no secret button that opens the Gateway to Hell.

It's just the vibration and rebound of the draught coming down the staircase.

You're disappointed. You go upstairs. In an empty pub, you order four pints of Becks and four double Southern Comfort and Lemonades. You give the astonishingly beautiful teenage girl, who looks like the angst-ridden suicidal high schooler from *American Beauty* (but they all do, don't they, they all do nowadays, they all look like her), a fifty pound note and she gives you a tenner and change back.

She gives you a tray, and it still takes you two trips.

C'mon, you. Let's get these ales down our neck.

Oh, man…

I insist.

You pick up a Becks, and you clink glasses with Beanie.

To the Pies, you say.

You down the pint in two gulps and one of the Southern Comforts. Beanie tries resolutely, to do the same, but fails. He runs upstairs to the toilet, where he informs you on his return that he was sick.

The hour passes, and you drink six of the eight drinks. You are buzzing. A text message is sent. The pair of you stand and salute each other one last time, finish the beers you have in front of you. You should feel unsteady, but you don't.

You haven't felt anticipation like this for fifteen years.

It courses through you and for a moment, your troubles seem like someone else's. You go to the toilet and look at yourself in the mirror. Your cheeks glow and your eyes shine.

You begin to laugh.

Beanie throws up, but neatly, and mops his mouth with toilet roll.

He's gone silent.

It was always like this.

It has always been like this.

You see the young lads outside the Galleria where the Flying Horse used to be. About ten of them. Beanie tells you there are more than that, but everyone has split up. You don't know any of them, but Beanie shakes hands and introduces you.

They're not happy with the turnout of old boys. They make that clear. For a brief moment, you don't know why you're there. You're a fish out of water. You have never felt as out of place as this in your life, and then the moment passes.

You begin the walk to Broad Marsh and to your destiny. You turn your iPod on.

The Bends by Radiohead.

Beanie points out several men you half know, and he's pleased. Some old fuckers have joined in after all! He says. You don't know them well.

One of them is an old punk. Another is from Bilborough.

You walk through the doors to Broad Marsh and through the open plan concourse, past the ambulance chasers and the chuggers and the arcades for the kids, the Outrun machine and the House of the Dead.

By Argos you see Crumble and some of the new school, and Paul from Bestwood, and some of the Newark lot, Whisky Jack, who both come up to you and shake your hand.

There's some Forest with us, Beanie says, knowing you probably won't approve, but it's not the same world, and you shrug your shoulders.

The young mix in a way old Notts never did.

You walk down the subway, past the King John, now boarded up and ruined. Beanie tells you all to turn into the bus station. You do so. He's grinning.

Look at this blast from the past, he says.

Two familiar figures sit on a bench.

You never expected to see them, and you speed up and trot past the young uns, who wouldn't recognise the significance of what they were now part of.

One, still as big as ever, at least twenty stone, wearing a smart combat jacket, jeans and boots. He's doing something with his Blackberry, and if the rumours are true, you realise if he's part of this, he has more to lose than anyone does.

The other is smaller, and you're taken aback when you see him.

He's frail, half his old size. He looks like he would blow away in the wind. He isn't smoking. He takes a fraction of a second longer than you'd expect to get off his seat. You feel the urge to hug them both, but you're not sure how they'd take that, so you don't.

Older Bully looks at you. His face is parchment coloured, eyes the colour of sour milk.

I've been in training for this, he says. Gym every night. Lentil stew and plenty of five-a-day. Look at how well it's worked.

Younger Bully grins. I heard you were coming. Couldn't let you get beat up like you usually do, he says.

Hands are shaken. You feel a bit tearful, but you suppress it. The nostalgia is pungent.

You're tapping into something.

Beanie taps you on the shoulder.

He shows you a text message; the number 10 with a smiley face. The cunts are here, he says. They'll be at the meet in ten minutes. Come on, we don't have much time.

He drops two more text messages and puts his phone away. There are about thirty of you, with another fifteen already in the Meadows on the other side of the station. You're going to meet them at the old Hicking's Factory back entrance. With any luck, you'll time it right and ambush the enemy from two sides. Cut them to pieces.

Maps have been exchanged in advance on Linkedin, the names of two companies.

Crumble's idea to use Linkedin. No monitoring by filth. You split up into fives. You hope there are no coppers because all this angst would be for nothing, all this soul searching, all this madness, though Beanie is sure there'll be none - there haven't been all season because Notts don't want to pay for it, and football has become a game for the middle classes who don't fight.

You hang back and walk with the Bullys while Beanie walks ahead, past the train station. Older Bully looks about sixty, and he is struggling to walk without coughing. There is a stench of death about him, which makes a change from the stench of fags. *He is here to die*, you think, like the ancient Indians who leave the tepee in the barren winter to die in the snow, thus preserving the resources of the tribe.

A dignified death.

Still he grins.

Why would he die in his stinking pit when he can die with a sword in his hand?

You walk past the station concourse, past the homeless and the travellers, and the long line of green taxis and the bright-eyed students with rucsacs the size of wheely bins, setting out into the big wide world - carrying their ambitions on their sleeves.

I'm going to be famous, mum.

I'm going to be rich, dad.

I'm going to end up running a branch of a multi-national company.

If I work hard, I'll be successful.

If I get my degree, I'll be somebody.

Globalisation and overproduction of graduates means that only one in a hundred will ever be as successful as they believe they will be. It's sad, mad, and bad. You're glad you aren't graduating in 2012.

You've had your life. If you die, who cares.

You've got your memories and achievements to take to Hell with you. You've lived and loved, and no one lives forever. You walk briskly past determinedly. Down past the new multi-storey car park foundations at the back of the train station. You think about how stupid all this is, this madness; how, if you get caught, they'll laugh at you in the papers. The magistrate will laugh at you, say that you should know better at your age, and you'll struggle to get a new job because they all want enhanced CRBs, and all the other shit that obsesses you.

Worse, you could get stabbed, because the young ones use decorator's knives and Stanley's, and custom-made blades that are easy to hide and they have the capacity to tear you to pieces. They've even resurrected the twin-blade strategy so beloved of old school Scallies - the twin Stanley blades separated by a thin piece of blu tac, which, after contact with six inches of ruddy cheekbone, make it virtually impossible for the surgeon to stitch the serrated flesh back together.

That would be some barrier in an interview.

But you don't care.

You *should* care, but you don't. You don't care if you get nicked, or battered, or brain damaged, or stabbed, or humiliated in the courts because you're too old for this; you don't care.

You don't care.

You don't even care if you die. You're buzzing because you're with people who've never let you down.

Unlike the kids who battered you at school.

Unlike your teachers.

Unlike your wife.

Unlike your son.

Unlike your employer.

The tribe.
Notts County FC
Always there.

The worst thing of all, the very worst thing, is that when Rita called you on Wednesday night she told you that she had met someone else.

Up until five minutes ago, you felt nothing, nothing. You thought you were incapable of feeling. You know that when you do start to feel something about *that* situation, about Rita, it's going to be bad, really bad, *really, really* bad, and you'd rather not face that because you still love her, and you always will.

She doesn't give a fuck about you.

Last night, the night before, and the night before, she'll have been with that someone else, and when your emotions return, along with the ability to *see* and to *imagine,* the pain will be indescribable. If they return.

You wonder who he is, but you will never want to know. In a strange way, she loved you when you were a football hooligan, and she may love you like she used to when she hears you led a charge into sixty northern hooligans with a reputation for pathological violence.

(My hero!)

Maybe that was what was missing all along.

You know you're just being stupid.

She's gone.

You turn the corner. Everyone gathers next to a chain-link fence surrounding waste ground and an old factory.

It's an impressive turnout. Beanie tells you all to shush, but that's not necessary. You're all too nervous to talk. You can see the others come down Lawrence Road. Ten or eleven of them in hooded jackets. Dark jackets.

It's not as colourful nowadays.

There are no lilacs.

The tension is electric.
You and the Bullys move to the front.
Just like the old days.
It's eighty degrees and you're not perspiring.
You are calm.
You are at peace.
(It's my turn.)
Then you see them.
You hear someone say, fuck me, there's hundreds of the cunts.

Someone else says, So! Keep your cheeks together.

They come from behind the van rental place you used to get to Swansea, and they start to walk toward you.

They can see both ways along the route they are taking; the ambush plan is a dud.

You wonder whether Beanie expected this.

There are anywhere between sixty and a hundred.

Designer gear, the modern stuff.

Non Vintage.

Dark colours. Hoods.

Bad trainers.

There are no pastels.

There are no Gazelles.

No Borg Elites.

A new world.

The modern world.

Tooled up.

You can see the metal of their weapons flash in the sunlight.

Car aerials and crowbars, and Stanleys and decorator's knives, and coshes and brass-knuckle dusters.

You remember York and the golf umbrellas with sharpened nibs.

Leather pouches stitched full of ball bearings.

A machete.

Nunchacku.

Shuriken.

Someone has fashioned a club from half a metre of armoured cable.

Another has secreted a Kyocera in his sock. An instrument of permanent ultra violence capable of severing joints with one silent swoosh.

Bricks.

Glass bottles split and jagged in two.

You are not afraid.

You head to your death, and you are not afraid.

No pain.
Rita.
There is silence. Complete silence.
Everything is still. You fan out across the road.
You hear shouting.
Distinct. Louder and louder.
(C'mon then!)
You hear someone scream.
Berserker screaming.
You tap Older Bully on his shoulder.
He looks completely content.
Younger Bully grins, clenches his fists.
Beanie, also.
Crumble.
Basford Paul.
Whisky Jack.
The young uns.
None of them show any sign of running.
Their baptism.
Their confirmation.

At that precise moment, you feel completely content.

Completely.

One with the universe.

You are finally home.

The invaders trot toward you, and even though the afternoon sun is behind them, you can see their faces.

Stamford Bridge.
Stamford Bridge.

It communicates through the group, without words.
Beanie makes a subtle gesture.

And…
…you…
…charge…

About the Author

Mark Barry, author of *Hollywood Shakedown*, the highly acclaimed *Carla* and the top selling *Ultra Violence,* is a writer and publisher based in Nottingham and Southwell.

He writes extensively on a variety of topics including, horseracing, football, personality disorders and human relationships, but most recently, he writes about life in Nottingham and monitors closely its ever changing face.

Mark has been interviewed on several Radio chat shows where he has given readings of his work. His writing has been featured in the national press, and he has also been interviewed on television.

Mark resides in Southwell, Nottinghamshire and has one son, Matthew.

Printed in Great Britain
by Amazon.co.uk, Ltd.,
Marston Gate.